John Martineau

**Letters from Australia**

John Martineau

**Letters from Australia**

ISBN/EAN: 9783744718752

Printed in Europe, USA, Canada, Australia, Japan

Cover: Foto ©ninafisch / pixelio.de

More available books at **www.hansebooks.com**

**Edmund Potter,**
  **Camfield Place.**

# LETTERS

## FROM

# AUSTRALIA.

BY

JOHN MARTINEAU.

LONDON:
LONGMANS, GREEN, AND CO.
1869.

# PREFACE.

THE following Letters were most of them written in Australia in 1867, and were published in the *Spectator* in the course of that and the following year. Some are reprinted without alteration, others have been added to and altered, and others are new.

No attempt has been made to mould them into a continuous or complete account either of the past history or present condition of the three colonies which they endeavour to describe. Those of the colonies which are old enough to possess a history have had it already written. And as for their present state, it would be presumptuous to suppose that fifteen months divided between them could have sufficed to enable me, circumstanced as I was, to give anything like a complete account of countries so large, or to obtain an accurate understanding of all the various political questions and phenomena presented by them. The organisation of school education, for instance, for which I am told some of the Australian legislatures deserve credit, was a matter that did not come under my notice, and important as this question is now becoming, I am unable to import any evidence bearing upon it.

In the absence of any exciting personal adventures there was no excuse for writing a diary or personal narrative. I was not even stopped by bushrangers; though had I wished it, and made my wishes known, 'Thunderbolt' would doubtless have been delighted to 'stick up' the Scone and Singleton Mail the day I was in it, instead of two or three days later, and again about a fortnight afterwards.

But a single day, a single hour spent in a new-world colony dissipates many delusions, and conveys many facts and ideas and impressions of it, which no amount of reading or of second-hand information can altogether supply, and which ought to confer the power of presenting a more vivid and real picture than a mere compiler at a distance can give.

These letters are therefore published, fragmentary as they are, for what they are worth. They aim at being accurate as far as they go, even at the expense of being in the last degree dull.

I am afraid we English are indolent and apathetic upon political questions, however important, unless there is the amusement and relish of party-spirit or religious excitement to make them palatable. Hitherto the want of interest taken by England in her colonies has been as remarkable as it is unfortunate. Even the discovery of gold, and all the strange and interesting scenes and events which it produced, dispelled this want of interest only for a time. But some day or other, it is to be hoped, we shall wake up to the significance of the fact that tens of thousands of able-bodied paupers are being supported in idleness, while *some* at least of the colonies are, under certain conditions, offering free passages to those who will go to them. If we think about this fact and its surrounding circumstances, we may reflect that to ignore such questions for the sake of discussing a 'free breakfast-table,' or even an alteration of the franchise, is rather like fiddling while Rome is burning.

Sooner or later England may be forced to take a keener interest in these matters. Pressing as is the need for emigration, to carry it out effectually is not so easy a matter as appears at first sight. Colonial questions and difficulties of the utmost delicacy and importance may arise at any time. There is a floating population of gold-diggers in Australia with few or no permanent interests in any one colony or country. The discovery of a rich gold field in any new locality would attract them from all quarters and make them a majority for the time being of the population of the colony in which they are, and as such the dictators of the policy of its government. What that policy might chance to be no one can say, or how it might bear upon immigration. In Victoria there appears, unfortunately, to be a growing disposition to discourage it. It is to be hoped that if any necessity for critical action should arise we may have a Colonial Secretary competent and willing to take the straight course and do the right thing, to the extent of such power as still remains to him, without too much deference to uninstructed public opinion.

I have seen more of Tasmania than of Victoria or New South Wales, and have had access to more sources of information concerning it. On account of its natural features it is the pleasantest, politically it is at present the least important of the three. Victoria presents the most characteristic example of the working of extreme democratic institutions. There, if anywhere, owing to the exceptionally general dispersion amongst all classes of men of intelligence, education, and general experience, they have had a favourable field, and there, if one may trust one's eyes and ears and the opinion of those best qualified to judge, they have produced the most deplorable results. Since these letters were written, an article called ' Democratic Government in Victoria ' appeared in the *Westminster Review* for April 1868, evidently written by one who has a close acquaintance (to which I can lay no claim) with the minutiæ of

Victorian political life. That an article so able, and describing a condition of things so startling and so new to people in England, should not have attracted more attention there, is a striking instance of our apathy to anything about the colonies. In Melbourne it created such a sensation that there was a rush to obtain the *Review* at almost any price; it was reprinted, and lectured upon, and became one of the chief topics of interest. Those who care to know what the Legislature is like in Victoria, those who would learn to what ultra-democratic institutions at any rate *may* tend, should read this article. What little my observation had enabled me to say on the same subject before its appearance is now scarcely worth reprinting, except as corroborative testimony (so far as it goes) of a wholly independent observer (for I am ignorant even of the name of the writer). ' One result of the system which in Victoria seems to be a necessary outcome of manhood suffrage ' (says the writer)

' is to exclude any man of inconveniently refined temperament, of a too fastidious intellect, and an oppressively severe independence of opinion, from any part in the representation of the colony. At the present time, it may be said, without any exaggeration, that no such man has the smallest chance of being elected, however liberal may be his opinions, and though he may be a staunch democrat, as democracy is understood in Europe, by any of the larger constituencies of Victoria, outside of the metropolis itself. The candidate who is preferred is the man who has nothing—who is not independent, who is not fastidious, who is not in any way particular or remarkable. Upon such a blank the democracy is able to impress its will most fully. . . . .

. . . . 'As a rule when two men are opposed to each other at an election, in three out of four of the Victorian constituencies, the worse man, the more ignorant, the less honest, and the more reckless is chosen.' (Pp. 496, 498.)

That is to say, the system is not only the opposite of an aristocracy of birth, wealth, talent, or merit, it is not only the repudiation of hero-worship in any form—even of that lowest form of it, the worship of the demagogue of the hour—but it is a deliberate attempt to set up what the world has not yet had occasion even to coin a word for—*Kakistocracy*, a Legislature composed of the meanest and worst, chosen as such.

Bad legislation is not the sole or the worst consequence of all this. Far worse is the demoralization with which political life is infected. The very idea of right and wrong, true and untrue, in politics, is in danger of being lost sight of. *L'État c'est moi*, said Louis Quatorze, and acted accordingly. *Ego sum Imperator Romanus et super grammaticam,** said an old German Emperor, when an imperfection in his Latinity was hinted at. 'The majority of the Colony is on our side, and the will of the people is above all

---

* Carlyle's *Frederick the Great*.

rules of right and wrong,' said (in effect) the Administration of Victoria during the late 'Darling-grant' crisis, being too obviously and palpably in the wrong to use any other kind of argument. And for the time being Louis Quatorze was for many purposes the State, Henry the Fowler's Latin went uncorrected, and Mr. Higinbotham still bears sway by virtue of his majority. But the Bourbon *régime* is no more, the principles of Latin Grammar remain in spite of any German Emperor, and the doctrine of the infallibility of majorities may likewise in its turn pass away. Sooner or later a democracy is likely to get weary of its puppet delegates, and to revert to the instinct which prompts men to follow strength rather than to drive weakness. The real fear is not so much lest democracy should become stereotyped and permanent in its present condition, as that the legislature, demoralised and weakened by corruption, should some day fall a too easy prey to despotism exercised by some strong unscrupulous hand, and aided perhaps by some one of the colossal fortunes, such as are being accumulated there, and which their possessors have as yet found few opportunities of spending. What form of government can be so unstable, so easily overturned as a corrupt ptochocracy?

There are those who admitting all these evils refuse to connect them essentially or in any degree with the extreme democratic nature of the institutions of the colony. Political results are not traceable and demonstrable like a proposition in Euclid; but it is useless to attempt to ignore the broad fact pointed out in the review already quoted, that legislation has become worse and corruption more rife as the democratic element has been more and more developed. Objectionable as a plutocracy is in theory, it is undeniable that the Legislative Council, which is chosen by electors possessing freehold worth 1000*l.* or 100*l.* a year, or being lawyers, clergymen, &c., has been composed of members superior beyond all comparison in character and ability to the members of the House of Assembly which is chosen by manhood suffrage. On the two most important questions of the day, the Darling grant and protection, the Upper House has been steadily right—in Australia outside the colony itself there is scarcely any difference of opinion as to this—and the Lower House persistently wrong. Still less is it to be denied that it is to the too great sensitiveness to public opinion, to the ready and even avowed willingness of the administration to trim its sails to every change of the popular wind, which is the direct consequence of a democratic constitution without proper checks, that many of the worst evils are attributable.

Others, again, there are who avowedly profess kakistocratical principles (if I may be excused for using the word) and say that to place men of superior virtue or talent in a position of authority is to divert and control the natural tendency of the mass, which they consider to be always in the right direction; therefore that it is better that public men should be nonentities than guides or patterns. It is impossible to argue against such a position. One can only take issue upon it, and, pointing to facts, say that the tyranny of majorities over minorities is the form of tyranny most to be feared at the present time, one which may become very prevalent and very galling. At the last election in Victoria the candidates on the Opposition side polled 28,888 votes against 32,728 polled by the Ministerialist and popular party, that is, in the proportion of a little more than seven to eight; yet the result was only 17 Opposition, against 54 Ministerialist members.* The large minority did not obtain anything like an adequate representation, and but for the still greater preponderance in the opposite direction in the Upper House, which the popular party seek to abolish, it would have seemed to the world outside as if Victoria were all but unanimous in approving the extraordinary course which the Administration was pursuing.

Looking at these figures it is some small satisfaction to reflect that there is a minority-clause in our

* This excludes 7 members returned without a contest, and makes a total of 56 Ministerialists and 21 Opposition members, the 78th being (I presume) the Speaker and reckoned neutral. The figures are from the Melbourne *Argus*, February 1868.

English Reform Bill, which asserts, however imperfectly, the principle of representation of minorities. But however sound the principle may be, it will be hard to carry it out by any mere electoral device. No one, for instance, can doubt that there is a large and important and intelligent section of the community at the present time which is really and not only in name Conservative, and which sympathised with the seceders from the late Administration, General Peel, Lord Carnarvon, and Lord Salisbury. Yet at the elections just over not a single candidate raised his voice on their side, or ventured to hint at an opinion that the suffrage might have been unduly or unwisely extended. It is scarcely too much to say that the real Conservatives are almost unrepresented in the present House of Commons. It will be well if, as our constitution becomes more democratic, a larger and larger proportion of those who are most disinterested and best qualified to legislate or govern have not to make way, as has been the case in Victoria, for those who are willing to accept the servitude and the wages of the delegate.

Nor is there any security that democratic opinions will be the only ones for which constituencies will exact pledges. We have just seen the most disinterested and unselfish friend that the working-men of London possess in Parliament, in spite of his 'advanced' opinions, constrained to withdraw from contesting a large constituency mainly on account of his undiplomatically expressed preference for a just balance over a false one, and in the face of probable defeat to make way for nonentities who would preserve a prudent silence on such unpleasant topics.

All honour to those amongst our public men who hold popular opinions honestly, and prove their honesty by the consistency of their private lives. The danger is lest they should be swamped by those who having in reality no such convictions profess them with the greater ostentation. For the former are likely to be few in number. The genuine democrat, the man who is readiest to sacrifice himself for the mass, does not in general seek public life.

Those whose convictions are different, are none the less bound in honour to cling to them, because they involve (as far as can be foreseen) inevitable and perpetual political ostracism. It is indeed said, that whether an unmixed democracy be a blessing or not matters little; for it is ordained for us—as is plain enough—sooner or later, and all efforts can but stave it off for a time. It may be so. And it *may* be, at the same time, that it is coming because we have brought it down upon ourselves, invoked our own wholesome punishment, as the Jews did when they asked for a king to reign over them. It may be thus, and thus only, that the *vox populi* which demands democracy, and the *vox Dei* which grants and ordains it, are in harmony.* If Samuel was not ashamed to be so far 'behind the age' as to tremble at the decree, and to shudder at the thought of the sons and daughters of Israel becoming slaves to an oriental despot, may not some of us be justified in seeking at least to stave off some of the changes that seem to be in store for us, and in shrinking with abhorrence from the Nessus-robe of corruption which seems to be a prominent characteristic of ultra-democracy?

* See *Prophets and Kings*, p. 11. By the Rev. F. D. Maurice.

# CONTENTS.

|  |  | PAGE |
|---|---|---|
| I. | A Voyage to Australia | 1 |
| II. | Melbourne | 13 |
| III. | Ballarat | 26 |
| IV. | Squatting in Victoria | 35 |
| V. | Politics in Victoria | 50 |
| VI. | Tasmania | 59 |
| VII. | Tasmania (*continued*) | 71 |
| VIII. | Tasmania (*continued*) | 85 |
| IX. | Sydney and its Neighbourhood | 101 |
| X. | An Institution of New South Wales | 115 |
| XI. | Political Difficulties of New South Wales | 121 |
| XII. | Aristocracy and Kakistocracy | 132 |
| XIII. | Mother and Daughter | 149 |
| XIV. | Home Again | 162 |
| XV. | Change of Air | 180 |
| XVI. | A Plea for Australian Loyalty | 192 |
| XVII. | Loyalty and Cynicism | 200 |

## I.

### A VOYAGE TO AUSTRALIA.

SOME PEOPLE who have been to the Antipodes and back will tell you that a voyage to Australia in a good sailing ship is a very pleasant way of spending three months. Seen through the halo of distance it may seem so; certainly it leaves pleasant and amusing reminiscences behind. But I doubt if one person in twenty on board our excellent ship the *Mercia*, provided as she was with every comfort, or on board any other ship whatsoever, if cross-examined *during* the voyage, would have persisted that he was thoroughly enjoying it. From the first, a resigned rather than a cheerful look is to be noticed among the passengers. Even those who at starting were loudest in their praises of a sea life spoke in the same breath of finding means, and slender means they seemed, of relieving its tedium and monotony.

We left Plymouth in the fag end of a gale. The second day, just about the place where the *London* is supposed to have gone down, a large piece of timber was floating high out of the water. We passed within twenty yards of it, and I then saw it was the keel of a vessel, of three or four hundred tons, capsized, and drifting bottom upwards. There was still a good deal of swell, and it would have been dangerous as well as useless to lower a boat; so we passed it almost in silence, and in a few minutes it was out of sight astern.

For a week or so the cuddy and even the poop were almost deserted. By degrees the population emerged from their cabins like rabbits from their burrows, to the number of forty or more, so that there was scarcely room to sit at table. Most of the passengers are Australians, 'old chums,' who have crossed the Line more than once, and are going back, either because the east winds of the old country last too long and are too keen after an Australian sun, or because they have come to an end of their holiday. Even among second and third class passengers this is so, for the attraction homewards is still strong, and it is common enough, it seems, for clerks and persons holding mercantile situations to get a year's leave to go home. There are one or two brides, and about a dozen others, not yet Australian, some of them more or less invalids, taking the voyage for pure sea air's sake, and hoping by following the sun across the Line to enjoy three summers in succession. Six children and a nurse abide in one stern-cabin; the other has been fitted up luxuriously and artistically with cushions, pictures, and loaded book-shelves, by a man who apparently intends to pass the time in literary retirement in the bosom of his family. Alas! in the stern there is motion on the calmest day. Not an hour is it possible to write or read there without experiencing certain premonitory symptoms necessitating an adjournment to the fresh air on deck.

It is not easy to be alone or to be industrious at any time on board ship. But it is not till you enter the tropics that exertion of body or mind seems to become impossible. It is then that your limbs almost refuse to move, your eyes to see, and your brains to think. The deck is strewn all day with slumbering forms. No plank, no hen-coop redolent of unpleasant odours, is so hard as to repel sleep. It is seldom that a sail needs setting or taking in. Even the barometer almost refuses to move, and influenced (it is said) only by the tide, sinks and rises almost inappreciably with lazy regularity. Nor is there often any excitement to arouse us. Twice only throughout the voyage is land seen: the rough jagged outline of Madeira, and the Desertas, rising from a smooth sheet of blue and purple water, and standing out against the glowing colours of the setting sun; and a few days later Palma, hiding the Peak of Teneriffe. We hope in vain to see, later on, Trinidad (the southern, not the West Indian, Trinidad) and Tristan da Cunha. There are two months in which the horizon is straight with a straightness abhorred on land by nature, such as even the deserts of Africa do not afford. Can it be that so much of the globe is always to be a dreary waste of waters? Is it all needed to make wind and rain, and to be a purifier of the land? Or when earth is overpeopled, will a new creation spring out of the sea? At any rate, there is change of some kind going on. We are unpleasantly made aware of this by a sudden cessation of wind, with calms, squalls, and foul wind, off the Canaries, in what should be the very heart of the trade-winds—the trades, whose blast used to be as steady and uniform as the course of the sun itself. A great change has occurred, says the captain ruefully, even in his time (and he is not forty,) in their regularity. If they go on at this rate, there may be none at all in a century, and not Maury himself can foresee the consequences of that.

On the other hand, the luck is with us when we come to the much-dreaded belt of calms, which lies near the equator, shifting north and south of it, according to the time of year, but always more to the north than to the south of it. Often are ships detained there for days, and even weeks, drenched in tropical rain, which makes it necessary to keep the skylights shut, to the great discomfort of everyone, except the ducks and geese, which are for the only time during the voyage released from their narrow coops, and put in possession of unlimited water and free range of the poop. For two or three weeks the thermometer stands at from 80° to 84°, not varying perceptibly day or night. In the upper-deck cabins there is plenty of ventilation—you may make them a race-course of draughts,—but below it is intolerable. It is unsafe to sleep on deck at night, for the air is charged with moisture. Portmanteaux, bags, hats, coats, and boots cover themselves with furry coats of green and blue mould. It is not unhealthy, but it is enervating and wearisome, except for five minutes soon after sunrise, when in the intervals of washing the decks the hose is turned upon you, as you stand thinking the warm air clothing enough. There is not much to look at but the flying-fish, as they rise in flocks, frightened from under the ship's bows, and tumble in again with a splash a hundred yards off; and at night the brilliant phosphorescence which lights up the white foam in the vessel's wake. For two days amongst the Madeiras turtles floated by asleep, but they were too wary to be caught.

It was a relief when one day, south of Trinidad, the air grew suddenly cooler, the flying-fish disappeared, and the first Cape-pigeon, and the first albatross, then Cape-geese, Cape-hens, and I know not what other birds, gave us hope that our voyage was half over, and that in ten days we might be in the longitude of the Cape. From hence till land was sighted some of these birds were always in sight of the ship. Sometimes four and five albatrosses at once were swooping about astern, some of them showing marks of having been struck with shot. It was useless to shoot at them, for they would have been lost; but we caught two with baited hooks, one measuring nine feet from wing to wing, and, unmindful of the 'Ancient Mariner,' slew and stuffed them.

I paid my footing on the forecastle, and hoped to see something of the crew. But one is apt to be in the way there, and it is difficult to know much of the sailors. Few realise—though it is a trite saying—how completely seafaring men are a race apart. Their habits.

ideas, wants, dangers, and hardships are almost unknown to landsmen. Seeing with one's own eyes how much hardship even now, and in the best appointed ships, occasionally falls to the lot of sailors, makes one aghast at the bare thought of what the miseries of a long voyage must have been in the old days before lime-juice and ventilation, and when the death or prostration of two-thirds of a crew from scurvy was quite a common occurrence. One begins to comprehend with amazement how the old discoverers must have had the souls of giants to sail month after month over unknown oceans and along unmapped coasts. Nor do landsmen realise how much loss of life there is at sea in merchant-ships, and how large a proportion of it is from preventible causes: how ships sail and are never heard of, and because there are no facts to make a story of, the papers scarcely mention it. Few but those in the merchant-service know how often, in order to save the expense of keeping ships idle in harbour, they are, after being fully insured, hurried to sea in utterly unseaworthy condition, with stores hastily put on board and so ill stowed that nothing is to be found when it is wanted, with crews engaged only the day before sailing, and consequently undisciplined, unknown to their officers, and frequently ill and useless from the effects of dissipation on shore, from the effects of which they have not had time to recover.* If the *London* belonged (as I believe it did)

---

\* See a remarkable pamphlet called *The Mercantile Commander, his Difficulties and Grievances.* Philip and Son, 32 Fleet Street.

to an exceptionally well-managed line of ships, how must it be with ships on ill-managed lines? It is true that a merchant-captain has it very much in its power to make his crew comfortable or miserable, and may often be a tyrant if he chooses. But it is also true that he is often very much at the mercy of his crew, amongst whom the chances are that he has at least one or two unruly and perhaps almost savage specimens. And with a new and strange crew every voyage, it is extremely difficult for him to establish and maintain discipline. He has very little power to punish, and in fact always does so at the risk of an action for assault at the end of the voyage. He often *dares* not put a mutinous man in irons because he cannot spare him; and it is sometimes only by sheer physical strength, by the knowledge that he could and would, if necessary, knock down any man in the ship who defied him, that he can maintain his authority. I have known a sailor after being some days in irons for mutinous conduct, say by way of an apology for his behaviour that hitherto he had always sailed in small ships, and had been accustomed, if he had a difference with his captain, to 'have it out' with him on the poop. A few days later the same man when drunk flew at the captain like a tiger, and had to be taken below and fastened to the main-deck like a wild beast, spread-eagle fashion, to keep him quiet.

Of the captain and officers, on the other hand, we see a great deal. Nothing can exceed their patience in listening to anything, reasonable or unreasonable, which the passengers have to say or to complain of, and in answering any questions, sensible or foolish. It is a hard, wearing, anxious life for them, requiring nerve, temper, and power of endurance. A ship often has only two responsible officers, so that each has at least half of every night for his watch on deck (in all weathers be it remembered) in addition to his work by day. Yet for this a chief officer gets the miserable pittance of 7*l*. a month, and a second mate and doctor 5*l*. a month, sometimes even less, ceasing immediately at the end of the voyage. One could wish that the great shipowners, wealthy as they must be, were a little more liberal in this respect. The butcher, on the other hand, is a man of capital, and comes furnished with a crowd of bull-dogs, canary-birds, thrushes, and other animals, which bring him in a handsome profit at the end of the voyage.

The *Mercia* is a sailing-ship, as all but two of the Australian ships are, and has no auxiliary screw. It is a real pleasure, for once, to be out of the way of steam-power, to be entirely at the mercy of winds and waves, and dependent on good old-fashioned seamanship. If a voyage lasts longer without steam, it is far more interesting and pleasant. There is an interest in seeing the sails worked, in pulling at a rope now and then. There is a little excitement in watching for a change of wind, in welcoming the moment in bad weather when the sensitive aneroid ceases falling and takes a turn, in anticipating a good or a bad day's run, in tracing the sometimes tortuous course on the chart, in speculating on the chance of an island being sighted or passed three or four hundred miles off. And in the morning there is something to be said about what the ship has done in the night; perhaps she has unexpectedly been put on the other tack, whereby somebody who had gone to sleep with his window open got a sea into his cabin. Or a sail has been split, or a spar carried away by a squall. All this is better at any rate than the everlasting monotonous throb of a steamer's screw, the uniform day's run which you can predict within twenty knots, the even sameness of the course drawn like a straight line across the ocean, and the smoke and smells of steam and oil (it is castor-oil) of the engines. And as for beauty, to stand by the wheel on the poop of a large ship, when the wind is light and fair and the studding-sails are set, projecting like wings over the ship's sides, and to look up amongst the towering curves of canvas and the maze of ropes and spars, is a very beautiful sight, a sight which tourists do not often see nowadays, and which in a generation or two, when the world is still more stifled with smoke and steam, may not be to be seen by anyone.

It is well if a voyage passes without quarrels among the passengers. In such close quarters, one must be inoffensive indeed to offend nobody. If you are cordial friends with a fat or unwashed man who has sat next you at three meals every day for three months, and with a loud voice insisted on being helped first to everything, your disposition must be amiable indeed. Except the relation between the two Lords Justices of the Court of Chancery, compared with which the bond of matrimony itself is a trifle, I know none so trying as close juxtaposition on board ship. You are at the mercy of the noisiest, the least scrupulous, and the most officious. If a man drinks, he will drink twice as much at sea, where he has nothing else to do. And you are lucky if you escape having one man at least among the passengers who drinks to excess.

However, eating, sleeping, or talking, we are always going; that is the great satisfaction. The average daily run greatly increases as we get south. Between 40° and 45° south latitude there are no more light or foul winds for a ship sailing east, and the course is straight, at the rate of about 250 knots a day. But it gets colder and colder, till one day, just as we are considering the chances of being carried to the south of Prince Edward's and Kerguelen Islands, the wind changes from north or north-west to south or south-west. It is equally fair for us, but we suddenly experience what it is to have a temperature of 40°, or lower, snow and hail falling, draughts as usual, and no possibility of a fire. It generally blows half a gale, sometimes a whole one. You cannot walk the deck to warm your feet, but must hold on fast, and take your chance of a drenching from one of the heavy seas, which from time to time strike the ship abeam, or on the quarter, with a noise like a ten-pound shot out of a gun. I cannot pretend to guess the height of the waves, but they are beyond comparison bigger than any I ever saw on the English coast. Standing on the poop, eighteen or twenty feet above the water, I have often seen the sun, when near its setting, *through* the clear green crest of a wave. For four or five days it is so misty and overcast that no observation of the sun can be obtained, and our position can be inferred only by 'dead reckoning.' Some seaweed has been seen. The currents are uncertain hereabouts, and even the position of the islands has, till within the last few years, been incorrectly laid down in the charts. So that the captain looks more harassed than usual, and does not leave the deck for long at a time, till at last we run into finer weather and see the sun again, and ascertain that we have been making a straight course in exactly the right direction and at a glorious rate.

And now the air gets daily clearer and drier; we are getting into the Australian climate. At last the day comes for sighting land. For an hour or more it is doubtful, then it is certain, that land is in sight. I put the day down as a red-letter day in my life, as we pass within a mile or two of Cape Otway, and see the red sandy cliffs, the pale green grass close to the water's edge, the lighthouse and telegraph station above, and behind, the ranges of thick impenetrable bush, huge forest trees, with their dark foliage standing out against the sky, a landscape as wild and unsullied by the hand of man as though it were a thousand miles from a settlement. One longs to be landed there and then, but the breeze is fair and strong, and though at sunset we take in all sail but topsails, we rush on, and are forced to heave-to before midnight, pitching and rolling in the swell, lest we get beyond Port Phillip

Heads in the night. Soon after midnight all are astir, for there is a rumour that the pilot is coming. A large star near the horizon is to be seen. It moves, gets larger; it is not a star; the moon's rays fall upon something indistinct on the waves beneath it, and shining white as silver a little schooner with a light at her mast-head shoots under the stern. The pilot climbs on board. Three more hours' pitching, and the long low Heads are left astern of us, and we are in smooth water. As the Melbourne folk are sitting down to their Sunday's breakfast, and those in England are going to bed for their Saturday night's rest, our anchor drops in Hobson's Bay, a mile or more from the long, low, sandy coast. Fronting us is Sandridge, the port of Melbourne; to the right, as far as the eye can see, dark green foliage, broken by clusters of houses and bare spaces of sand; and to the left, a marshy, sandy plain, bounded by the distant ranges, purple as the hills of Gascony or the Campagna.

## II.

### MELBOURNE.

'ALL I can see is my own, and all I can't see is my son's,' was the complacent remark, it is said, of John Batman, as he stood, some thirty-two years ago, looking over a vast tract of country which he thought he had bought as his own freehold from the aborigines for a few blankets and tomahawks. That tract of country comprised the ground whereon now stands Melbourne, nearly if not quite, the largest city in the southern half of the globe; in importance, actual or prospective, in the first rank of British cities.

Truly English it looks as yet, at first sight at any rate. After a long, wearisome voyage, the first impression is almost one of disappointment at having come so far only to see sights and hear sounds so familiar. Long before you land, the familiar ugly staring letters, with which the British shopkeeper delights to deface his dwelling, are visible on the waterside houses. A commonplace railway-train, with two classes to choose between, not one only, as might have been expected in a land of democracy, receives you at the shore end of the long wooden pier. You are set down in ten minutes in Melbourne itself, amongst cars, shops, hotels, and all the external appliances of old-world civilisation. But this first impression soon passes away. Already before entering the city itself, a white plain, marshy in winter, dried up and arid in summer, has been passed over. It is dotted over with little one-storied wooden houses, of which the verandah seems to be the most important part, and which are more like the mushroom erections on the sand *dunes* of Arcachon in the *landes* of Gascony than any habitation on English soil. And I suppose there is no spot in Melbourne where a man waking up, as from an enchanted sleep, and ignorant where he was, could for a moment fancy he was in England.

From the railway station you enter at once into the heart of the town. You pass into fine, straight, generally sloping streets, which will compare favourably with those of any English provincial town for width, for the number of well-filled showy shop-windows, and for the ambitious and costly architecture of the public buildings, hotels, and especially banks, which last are always numerous and conspicuous in Australian towns. First in importance among them is Collins Street, the Regent Street of Melbourne. Parallel, and scarcely inferior in rank to it, is Bourke Street, and at right angles to these are Elizabeth Street and four or five more which may be said to come next in dignity. These and several narrower ones, most of which are quiet and dignified and full of merchants' offices, make up the most important part of Melbourne proper, as distinguished from the suburbs, each of which, though an integral part of the capital, has a sort of separate existence of its own, and bears a relation to it more resembling that of Kensington or Hampstead to London, than that of Marylebone or Mayfair. This central part of the town is the original and old part, if it may be so called in comparison to the rest. It was planned out long before Melbourne was a populous or important city, in the days when Governors ruled as well as reigned, and was systematically laid out in alternately broad and narrow roadways. It was intended that only the broad ones should have houses built along them, the narrow ones being meant only for back entrances to the gardens and outbuildings which were to occupy the intervening space. But both have now long since been turned into streets of contiguous houses.

The lowness of the houses strikes a new comer from England as a feature which makes the general appearance of the city different from anything at home. Even in the heart of it, where space is so valuable that one might have expected it would be more economised, the houses have generally only one story above the ground floor, and in the suburbs often not even that. This is made all the more conspicuous by the width of the streets. These are not paved but are well macadamized, and are now in good order in all weathers; but on each side of them you have to cross by little bridges, if you are on foot, or if you are driving, to bump down into and through broad, deep, paved gutters, or rather water-courses full of running water, which exhibit nature not yet quite submissive to civilization. After heavy rain, torrents of water rush down them to such an extent that boats are sometimes required in some of the lower streets. There is a tradition that before Flinders Street was macadamized the mud was so deep there that a baby jolted out of a car was drowned in a rut before it could be picked up. In the principal thoroughfares the traffic on the foot-pavement is considerable enough, and indicates a large and busy population. But the roadway looks rather empty. In an afternoon you may see a good many buggies and a few English-looking carriages driving about; but there is never anything approaching to a continuous string of vehicles of any kind in motion. There are plenty of street-cars, or jingles as they are called, which are like Irish cars with the seat turned breadthways instead of lengthways, and with a covering to keep off sun and rain. Here and there are to be seen stands of drays waiting to be hired, as if the population were in a chronic state of change of domicile.

The wind and blinding sun make one wish that the streets were a little less straight, both to add to their picturesqueness, and so as to afford a little more shelter. Whether the keen wind in winter or the hot wind of summer be blowing, the lee-side of a wall is equally desirable. In summer after a day or two of parching hot wind from the north, the south wind will suddenly come into conflict with it, producing what is called a 'Southerly Buster'—a whirlwind full of dust, filling the air and darkening the sky, and resulting always in the victory of the south wind, and in a fall of temperature of twenty or thirty degrees in less than half an hour. But if curved streets are in some respects desirable, it must not be at the expense of a peculiar and most attractive feature in those of Melbourne, namely, that many of them have at each end a vista of open sky or distant mountain ranges, which in the clear dry air are always blue and distinct, and give a sense of space and freedom not common in the midst of large cities.

The respectable Briton everywhere clings to his black hat and black coat with tenacity. But the summer heat of Australia is too much for him, and white hats, or felt ones with stiff falling brim, and thick white pugrees give a semi-Indian look to the population. Those who have to do with horses, whether stockmen from the bush or livery-stable helpers, are particularly unlike their type in England. Instead of being the neatest and most closely buttoned and closely shaved of men, they will perhaps wear no coat or waistcoat, a purple flannel shirt, white linen inexpressibles, dirty unpolished jack-boots, a cabbage-tree hat, and a long beard. Follow one of them into the great horse-yard in Bourke Street, the Melbourne Tattersall's. The broken horses are first sold, very much as they might be at Aldridge's. Then the auctioneer goes to an inner part of the yard, where in large pens, strongly built of timber and six or seven feet high, is a 'mob' of a hundred or more four-year-old unbroken colts huddled together and as wild as hawks. Bidders climb up on to the railings and examine them as well as they can from there, for it is no easy matter to go amongst them or to distinguish one from the rest. The auctioneer puts them up for sale separately, and somehow or other, with much cracking of whips, each as his turn comes is driven out from among the rest into a separate pen. Probably the best of the mob had been picked out previously, for the commonest price at which I heard them knocked down was seventeen shillings and sixpence a-piece, and it is difficult to believe that, cheap as horses are in Australia, a good colt could be worth so little as that.

The space covered by Melbourne and its suburbs is, compared with an English or European town, out of all proportion large for the population. Short suburban railways, running all through and about it, make it easy for people to live at some distance from where their work is. Between one suburb and another there are often dreary spaces of bare ground, destitute of grass, and dusty or muddy according to the season. The population in some places is so sparse that you may have to wait some minutes if you want to ask your way of a passer-by. There is a so-called street, quite unknown to fame, rejoicing in the name of Hoddle Street (why Hoddle, and who or what Hoddle was, I have no idea), which cannot be much less, I should think, than three miles long. One end of it passes through a large, poorly-built suburb, called Collingwood; it then emerges into open ground and passes through some meadows by the river-side, which in a flood are sometimes many feet deep in water. For want of a bridge it (or rather its continuity or identity) crosses the river in a punt, and, still being Hoddle Street, forms part of South Yarra, a locality which disputes with Toorak the honour of being the Belgravia or Mayfair of Melbourne. Emerging from South Yarra it enters a sandy flat near the sea-shore, and ends its career (I believe, for I never followed it so far) somewhere in the pleasant sea-side suburb of St. Kilda.

The foreign element in Melbourne is very small. There are few Germans and fewer French. Only the Chinese are noticeable for their numbers. One meets them in the streets looking quite at home there, not begging, as in Europe, but prosperous and industrious. It is said that there are twenty thousand Chinamen in Victoria alone. One narrow street in the middle of Melbourne is inhabited almost exclusively by them, and is conspicuous with quaint blue and gold sign-boards covered with Chinese characters, looking like a large bit of tea-caddy, the proprietor's name being put up in English letters underneath, for the information of outer barbarians. Sun-kum-on is a very conspicuous name on one of the wharves at Sydney. Public opinion, which was very hostile to the Chinese at one time, seems to have rather turned in their favour. In New South Wales there was an Act of the Legislature excluding them, but it has lately been repealed. They do work which other people despise, and by their abstemious and parsimonious habits will slowly get rich on gold-fields abandoned by other diggers as worked out. As market-gardeners, they have done a real service to the Melbourne people. Formerly there were few if any vegetables to be had there in summer. It was supposed to be too dry and too hot to raise them. But by elaborate irrigation, unstinted spade labour, and abundant application of manure, the Chinese raise crop after crop of vegetables at all seasons, and in all soils. I saw two acres of ground in one of the suburbs which had been left uncultivated, and was altogether improfitable, till five Chinamen rented it for 25*l.* a year, and now they contrive to raise 300*l.* worth of garden produce yearly. They are a race living quite apart. They do not bring their wives with them from China; there are not more than three or four Chinese women in all Victoria, it is said. And the poorest of the poor of other races, probably with good reason (as one's nose suggests), will not live with them, much less intermarry with them.

The great and ever-present charm of Melbourne consists in the exceptionally vigorous and active appearance of its population. This is due simply to the fact that the great bulk of it was formed by the almost simultaneous immigration of men who are not yet grown old. As yet there are comparatively few old people to be seen about; and everybody seems hard at work and able to work. An immense majority of the grown-up men and women were born and bred in England. Many whom one meets about the streets look as if they might have a history of their own, full of interest and strange adventure, none perhaps more than the car-drivers, an occupation followed by some who have been used to a very different position in life. I never drove in a car without asking all I dared, and speculating as to what the reason was in each case for wandering to the Antipodes. Physically the Melbourne people are likely to be above the average; for, in the early days of the colony at least, the sick and weakly in constitution did not think of committing themselves to the then uncertain hardships and discomforts of a voyage and a new country. A certain degree of force of character too is probable in those who have had resolution enough to break through home ties and cast their lot in another hemisphere. Hence also in some respects the tie with the old country is a closer and firmer one than in most of the other Australian colonies. There is quite a crowd and an excitement about the post office for some time before the English mail closes. Little stalls are erected by newspaper-sellers, provided with pen, ink, and cover, to direct and despatch the newspapers to friends at home, and a brisk trade they seem to do. Home associations and reminiscences underlie and prevail over more recent ones. Even the word 'colonial' is often used to express disparagement; 'colonial manners,' for instance, is now and then employed as a synonym for roughness or rudeness.

In nothing is the energy and enterprise of the Melbourne people more conspicuous than in their public works. Lately, indeed, either money has not been so plentiful or else the desire of building has been less ardent, for many buildings have been left unfinished and in very unsightly plight. But the Postoffice *is* finished, and is a really magnificent building in its way. On the Legislative Council and Assembly Chambers an incredible amount of pains and money must have been expended, though perhaps with hardly adequate result. The architecture of the public buildings generally, if not always successful or in the best taste, is on the whole at least as good as in the average of public buildings at home; though it is disappointing to find that new requirements of climate have failed to inspire any originality of style or design, such as one sees growing up naturally and spontaneously in private houses, whether suburban villas or stationhouses in the bush.

But the institutions of the Museum, the Public Library, the Acclimatisation Gardens, and the Botanical Gardens, are above all cavil and beyond all praise. The last two in particular, aided as they are by a favourable climate, promise before many years are over to equal anything of the kind anywhere. Last and greatest of all is the great Yan-Yean Reservoir, which from twenty miles off pours its streams into the baths, fountains, gardens, and dusty streets of the thirsty city. Every house has its water-meter, and the price is only a shilling for a thousand gallons. Without this generous supply the suburbs would in summer be a Sahara, with a few dismal, almost leafless, gum-trees, instead of being brightened by pleasant gardens, enriched with English as well as semi-tropical flowers and fruits. The stiff clay, which is a quagmire in winter, dries up in summer like a sun-baked brick. Garden lawns are with difficulty kept green by Yan-Yean water turned on, not at intervals, but continuously through a perforated pipe. Yet the grass two or three feet off is quite dry. The water escapes through the first crack and is gone.

On the other hand, one soon experiences that a Circumlocution-Office is a Victorian quite as much as a home institution. Goods of all kinds, including passengers' luggage, are brought up by railway from each ship as it arrives, and discharged into a vast shed at the Melbourne railway station; and as there is now a tariff on most manufactured articles, nothing is allowed to leave the shed till it has been more or less inspected. Many hours did it take to select my various needles from this great bundle of hay, but it was not till my two saddles turned up that any difficulties were made about releasing them. On seeing them, a very young clerk in a cloth cap at a high desk referred me to a white-haired superior official, who shook his head and refused to let the saddles pass without an order from the commander-in-chief of the shed, who inhabits an office at its extreme end. Alas! the commander-in-chief, though the most courteous and obliging of men (as were indeed all the officials with whom I had to do that day), pronounced that I must ' pass an entry '—I think that is the expression—at the Custom-house. So to the Custom-house, a quarter of a mile off—the ugliest erection that ever was built or left half-built—I trudged. Going into a large hall I addressed a clerk, who gave me into the care of another clerk, who took me downstairs, and introduced me to a Custom-house agent, and then the real business began. Dictating to him, I made an affirmation to the effect that the saddles were old and for my own personal use, which affirmation having been, after one or two unsuccessful attempts, made in precise accordance with the facts of the case and duly signed, Custom-house agent, affirmation, and I walked upstairs to the ante-room, and at length to the sanctum of some high official, who after gently cross-examining me vouchsafed to append his initials, whereupon Custom-house agent, affirmation, and I walked downstairs again to the place whence we had come. I suppose I looked a little weary—it was a piping hot day—at this stage of the proceedings, for the Custom-house agent reassuringly remarked that it would not take more than a quarter of an hour more, a statement hardly verified by the result. The next step was for the Custom-house agent to make a memorandum of the nature of my affirmation, to make a number of copies thereof (I did not count how many, but there must have been at least five), and to despatch them by messengers, whither or wherefore I know not, nor why so many, unless they were tentative, in hopes of procuring a favourable response from one out of many possible sources. Anyhow, a sealed letter did at last arrive from somewhere; it was handed to me; I left the building, made for the shed, and delivered it to the commander-in-chief, who wrote and gave me another missive to the white-haired clerk, who made it all right with the young clerk in the cap, who gave me a pass-ticket, which I gave to my drayman, who gave it to the porter at the yard gate, who allowed the dray to pass, and I and my saddles were free.

## III.

### BALLARAT.

Two hours' railway travelling will take you from Melbourne to Geelong, over rich, flat, grassy plains, with scarcely a tree, nothing but ugly posts and rails to break their outline. In summer these plains must be parched and dreary beyond description; but it is May now, and the autumn rains have made them green as an emerald and pleasant for the eye to rest on. Geelong is scarcely worth stopping at, unless to speculate upon why it is not Melbourne, and Melbourne it, as might have been the case—so superior in many ways is its situation—if its harbour bar had been cut through a few years sooner. During two more hours' railway you rise gradually, and emerge from a forest of ill-grown, scrubby gums, upon a large, undulating, irregular amphitheatre, surrounded by small hills. Seventeen years ago the locality was scarcely ever visited except by blacks, for it was covered with bush and unproductive. Now it is Ballarat, the fourth city in Australia. A strange, irregular, uncouth, human ant-hill it is, with its miscellaneous cells above, and its galleries beneath the ground. You may walk two miles and more, from east to west or from north to south, without getting fairly out of the town. The houses are of all sorts, shapes, and sizes, generally not contiguous, and the majority consisting of a ground-floor only. Most conspicuous are the hotels, and the banks, glorying in stone fronts and plate glass, as befits their dignity; for are they not suckers at the fountain-head, drawing the golden stream which, joining other rills, waters the whole world of commerce? Next door to one of these is perhaps a common log-hut, or a two-roomed cottage of corrugated iron, or a large shop stocked till its miscellaneous contents overflow through doors and windows, and are hung on hooks and pegs outside. Next to this, perhaps, and still in the heart of the town, may be an acre or two of ground covered with disgorged gravel and mud, in the midst of which, and at one end of a great mound twenty or thirty feet high, puffs and sobs a steam engine, as it works the shaft and puddles the produce of the gold mine beneath. It is easy to gain admittance to a gold mine, at least if the manager is satisfied that you are not a spy, and are not interested in the 'claim' which lies nearest this one, and with which it probably is, or will be as a matter of course, engaged in litigation as soon as the workings of either approach the boundary between them. Boundaries above ground are productive enough of disputes, but they are nothing to boundaries under ground. The richest harvest reaped by the Victorian bar is that of mining cases and mining Appeals. But there is not much to see in a mine. Down below I suppose it is not so very different from a coal mine (for the gold is far too minute in quantity to be visible), and not much cleaner. The operations at the surface consist simply in stirring and washing the mud and gravel with water in various ways till the gold settles at the bottom. But a good big panfull of some two thousand pounds' worth of the clean yellow gold is a pretty thing to see for once.

But the strangest place in Ballarat is an unsightly piece of ground on the slope of a hill, many acres in extent, which has been turned over, heaped up, scooped out, drained, flooded, undermined, perforated, shored up with timber, sifted, scarified, and otherwise tormented as Mother Earth never was tormented before. It is the remains of the old surface diggings, almost (if not quite) the first discovered, and the richest in all Australia, but long since worked out, and now deserted and dismal. It is a pity that no scribbling digger kept a journal during the first year or two after gold was found. Generally speaking, I believe the stories which are told of those days are strictly true. The reality was so strange, so different from any other condition of circumstances conceivable in this century, the crowds suddenly collected were so miscellaneous, and at first so entirely emancipated from all rule, precedent, or prejudice, that there was enough that was original and ludicrous without having recourse to exaggeration and caricature. I believe it is a fact, and no fiction, that a successful digger had a gold collar made for his dog, that he, like his master, might put aside his working dress and be magnificent for the rest of his days. It is a fact that another rode through

Ballarat with his horse shod with gold. To keep a carriage and pair was the great ambition of a digger's wife. There was a woman near Colac who lived in a common log-hut, with nothing but mud for floor, and a couple of stools and a bench or two for furniture. Outside the hut was the carriage, under a tarpaulin, and a pair of horses grazed near. For a year or more she was constantly to be seen on the road to Geelong. Her son drove, and she sat inside in silks and satins gorgeously arrayed, a short pipe in her mouth, and the gin bottle reposing on the cushion by her side.

One day at Ballarat a man rushed up to the police magistrate, his face livid, and speechless with excitement, so that the magistrate began to think he had just committed or witnessed a murder. At last he found words to express himself. He had come upon a nugget so big he could scarcely carry it, and dared not bring it in alone. Two or three of the police went back with him to help him, and he brought it in in triumph, followed by a procession of diggers. And indeed it *was* a nugget. It was about as big as a leg of mutton, and much the same shape, white lumps of quartz sticking to it like so much fat. It weighed a hundred and thirty-five pounds, and he was offered 5,000*l.* for it on the spot. He refused to sell it, and took it home to England to exhibit it. But it proved to be a nugget of expensive habits, and at last was sold to pay for its keep and lodging, and the finder ended, as so many finders of great nuggets ended, in poverty and wretchedness, and even madness.

At Ararat, fifty-six miles beyond Ballarat, the goldfields remain just as they were left by the diggers; and the claims are more in working order and less broken in than at Ballarat. Ararat is now a thriving township, containing perhaps 2,000 inhabitants. Twelve years ago there were 65,000 people there, digging or dealing with diggers. When the 'rush' began the stream of people and drays was continuous, the noses of each team of bullocks close to the dray in front of them, for the whole fifty-six miles, along a track on which, though the district is a thriving one, you will now hardly meet anything on wheels once in ten miles. Centuries may pass without obliterating the traces of these diggings. There is a broad belt of ground, two or three miles long, pierced by thousands of shafts thirty or forty feet apart, with mounds of white sand and gravel beside them. Most of the shafts are oval, four or five feet long, and about two or three wide. Little holes are cut alternately in the nearest pair of opposite sides, to act as steps for going up and down. Each shaft is neatly and cleanly cut, and as intact as if freshly made. All are deserted now; only a few Chinamen remain, laboriously gathering up the crumbs that are left, and contriving to live and save money where an Englishman could not subsist.

There were comparatively few men, gentle or simple, in Victoria when gold was first found who did not try their luck at digging for a greater or less time. Nevertheless, though so short a time has elapsed, is is hard to get a true conception of the state of things during the height of the gold fever. No two men had the same experience. One will tell you that nothing could be more quiet and peaceable and orderly than a concourse of men upon a newly found gold-field; that property and life were safe, and every man so eagerly and excitedly absorbed in his work as scarcely to take his eyes off it while daylight lasted, and impatient of nothing except interruption. Another will say he never stirred after sunset without an open knife in his hand, and will tell you (no doubt with truth) that hundreds, and even thousands, disappeared, whether murdered for their gold, drowned in a swollen creek, or lost and starved in the bush, no one knew or cared to enquire; for in all that crowd who would miss a lonely and friendless man? Not that the police, as far as their scanty numbers permitted, were otherwise than most efficient. In general they were on the best of terms with the diggers; and only in one serious instance, the diggers at Ballarat, considering themselves aggrieved, made armed resistance to the authorities. They formed an entrenched camp and were not dispersed till as many as a hundred of their number had been killed or severely wounded. If money came fast, it had to be spent fast too. Actual famine was with difficulty averted during the first winter. The country round was drained of supplies; provisions went up to fabulous prices. The diggers could not eat their gold; and it cost 100*l.* a ton to bring up flour from Melbourne, for the road was a quagmire like that from Balaklava to Sebastopol, and ninety miles long instead of seven. The carcases of the dead draught bullocks were alone sufficient to indicate the track to one if not to two of the senses.

But it is a mistake to suppose that gold-digging has been throughout a gambling occupation, offering a few prizes and many blanks, and pursued only by reckless men. The big nuggets soon came to an end, and on the other hand experience was gained, and digging became in the long run a tolerably certain and steady occupation, at which a strong man able to bear heat and cold, wet and fatigue, could in general make a pretty steady income, though not often a large one. Many have risen from comparative poverty to great wealth in Victoria, a few by owning sheep stations, many by steady devotion to business, some without any real exertion of body or mind, by the sheer accident of lucky speculations; but I have never heard of a really wealthy man who became so by digging for gold. Yet some have gone on persistently year after year, in New South Wales, Victoria, and New Zealand, when one field was worked out travelling to another. For there was a strong fascination in the freedom and romance of the life. I have seen the pale face of an overworked waiter at a large hotel light up with enthusiasm as he spoke of it. He had left England and come to Australia ill of consumption, as a last chance to save his life. Idleness did not mend him, he said, so off he went with the rest to the diggings. The first day his limbs would hardly bear him, but each day he got a little stronger, till at the end of four years he had saved 700*l*. and his life. He had been in very different climates—in New South Wales, Victoria, and Otago —but, strange to say, heat, cold, and wet only helped to cure him, and he never even caught cold, he said, as long as he eschewed a house and was faithful to canvas. Alas! in an unlucky hour he invested his savings in township land; the place did not succeed, and in a few weeks his investment was not worth as many farthings as he had given pounds for it. And it was too late to begin again.

It is over now, the wonderful age of gold, as well as the primitive pastoral age which preceded it. In place of diggers swarming like bees, dignified steam-engines draw the gold from the earth, not for those who toil with pick and spade, but chiefly for that throng of mining brokers, and idle, disreputable speculators who crowd the pavement of the Ballarat 'Corner.' Few make money by investing in mines. Of those who do, most have secret information; for there is much trickery mixed up with operations in mining shares, and hundreds have lost by them the savings of more prosperous times. Victoria is no longer the place for men with few possessions beyond youth and energy, and with an antipathy to a high stool in a merchant's office. Let not any brilliant or laborious young Templar doubt but that Melbourne and Ballarat solicitors, like English ones, have sons and sons-in-law, and that there, as at Westminster, interest and connexion are useful, if not essential, handmaids to brains and industry. Romance is at an end; capital has reasserted its sway, and pride of purse is triumphant. It needs must be so; and doubtless, on the whole, mankind gains. But it is difficult to love humanity in the abstract, and tastes and convictions will quarrel sometimes.

## IV.

### SQUATTING IN VICTORIA.

IT sometimes happens that the commonest circumstances of life in distant countries are scarcely realised at home because they are too much matter of everyday experience to be spoken about. I doubt whether people in England appreciate the fact that the greater part of Australia is, in its natural state, for eight or nine months in the year almost entirely destitute of water. To a new comer it sounds strange to hear an up-country Squatter remark that he has no water on his run yet, but he hopes he soon shall have. Although more rain falls in Victoria than in most parts of England during the year, there are hardly any springs, and few streams except the large rivers, which are few and far between, which run for any considerable portion of the year. Why the rain runs off so fast is not thoroughly explained, but its seems there is an incrustation of the subsoil which prevents the rain from penetrating to any depth. The creeks, as they are called, leave waterholes, some of which never dry up through the summer; but these, also, are far between; and so generally the first business of a Squatter in new country is to construct tanks to receive the rain-water from the roofs of his house and outbuildings, which is his drinking-water, and very good water it is; and the second is to build a dam from six to twenty feet high across the nearest hollow—for almost every hollow is a water-course after heavy rain—and in this way to make a reservoir containing water enough for his sheep to drink all the year round, and be washed in at shearing time. A dam is as much an essential appendage to a station as a barn is to a farmyard.

Probably it is this absence of moisture in the ground, and consequently in the air also, which makes distant objects in Victoria so marvellously clear, and gives such peculiarly brilliant colour to the landscape where the conformation of the ground admits of a distant view. I never saw such brilliant colouring anywhere in Europe. It is the one redeeming feature, without which the scenery, except in the mountainous districts, would be tame and dreary enough. The country is seldom undulating, as in Tasmania. The trees are generally small, stunted, and diseased, except on the ranges; the plains are almost destitute of any trees at all, and vegetation is scanty, except in early spring-time. There is a great plain extending for nearly a hundred miles westward of Geelong almost without a break, so flat and (unlike the fen country in England) so destitute of trees or other objects high enough to break the line of the horizon, that at the height of a dozen feet from the ground you may any day see a hill—and not a high hill either—full forty-five miles distant as the crow flies, looking not dim and misty, but a clearly defined blue patch upon the horizon.

To most people there is something intolerably desolate and repulsive in such a plain. Even to those who are most fond of open country it must be depressing under certain circumstances, notably during a rainy fortnight in winter, or on a hot-wind day in summer. But there is something indescribably grand and enjoyable in the continual contemplation of so vast a landscape. When the sun is high it is an expanse of turf, green in winter and brown in summer; but as the afternoon advances, earth and sky become faintly purple, and crimson, and golden; the colours deepen from half-hour to half-hour, till the sun sinks into its bed of turf in a gorgeous blaze of splendour. There are several shallow lakes upon the plain, some very large, and most of them salt. Coming suddenly upon one of them one evening from behind some little sand-hills which concealed it, the margin for some hundred yards in width dry and coated with mud and brine, no human being or habitation visible, and the full brilliance of the setting sun lighting it up, the scene was (except for the absence of mountains in the distance) singularly like the landscape in Holman Hunt's picture of the 'Scape-Goat.' It is a pity that this kind of scenery is spoiled by cultivation. Cut up into little pieces, a plain loses its vastness, while its monotony is increased.

It is a pleasant life to have a station up the country (but not too far up), at least for a man not over gregarious in his habits and tastes, and whose mind is not set on those pleasures of town life which seem to possess the greatest attractions for the majority of mankind. It may be ten or twenty miles to the next station, or nearest doctor, or post-office, or church: and the owner of the next station may happen to be illiterate and uncongenial, the doctor generally intoxicated when sent for, and the post-mistress so lonely and dull that it is a necessity to her, poor thing! to read your letters and communicate their contents to her friends. But nobody thinks much of distance; there are plenty of horses, good or bad, and by going a little further afield you may be better suited. Then people journeying up the country drop in occasionally for a dinner and a night's lodging. If the visitor is at all presentable he is entertained with the best the house affords. If he is a stock driver, or shepherd, or labourer, he is entertained at the overseer's or the men's hut. There are rather too many such visitors sometimes; nobody is ever turned away, and there are idle fellows pretending to be in search of work and refusing it when it is offered them, who go from station to station living upon the Squatters. The house is generally comfortable enough nowadays, usually built partly of bluestone, partly of wooden slabs, and with only a ground floor, a single sitting-room, and a great deal of broad verandah, which answers the purpose of a sitting-room in fine weather. People are beginning to take pains with their gardens, and there is generally a fair supply of vegetables to help down the mutton. There is always good bread, and damper has long since vanished from civilised regions. Near the house is the overseer's cottage, and a little way off is the men's hut. The latter is usually only a log hut, made of boards; it contains two rooms, a day-room and a dormitory, and looks comfortless enough. The furniture is a bench or two, a table, and perhaps a wooden arm-chair; and in the dormitory the only beds are wooden bunks, like ships' berths, built against the wall in two tiers. The unmarried men about the station live here, perhaps half a dozen in all. The head of the establishment is the cook, whose business it is to keep the hut and prepare the food. In the old, rough days he needed to be a man able to hold his own and preserve discipline, and if necessary to prove himself the better man against anyone who complained of the dinner. He is generally butcher and baker to the whole station. At a short distance off is the wool-shed, the most important and imposing building of all, where the sheep are shorn and the wool packed. And there are a few outlying shepherd's huts, each with its hutkeeper (unless the shepherd is married), whose only business is to cook and keep house for the shepherd, and occasionally lend a hand with the sheep pens. They all get good wages. The shepherds get from 40*l.* to 50*l.* a year, and the hutkeepers from 30*l.* to 40*l.*, and they get a sheep a week between two, and the other usual rations. Strange to say, the men do not seem to care for vegetables, and seldom take the trouble to make a garden, though they might have as much garden ground as they liked for nothing.

There is not often very much to do except for two or

three weeks at shearing time, when everything is once fairly set going. The toils and pleasures of stock-riding on cattle stations, of which we read in *Geoffrey Hamlyn*, are almost at an end in Victoria. For, alas! it is found more economical to divide the runs into paddocks by wire fences, and so to employ fewer shepherds or stock riders. And so, though you can see the place you want to ride to, or at any rate know in which direction to go, you must ask your way among the fences almost as if they were rows of houses. The black-fellows, and the wild dogs, and (except in thickly-wooded districts, where they are as numerous as ever) even the kangaroos are gone, which is an unmixed advantage for the Squatter, if not for idle and inquisitive friends who stay with him. Near a forest you may see scudding about little white clouds, which, on closer inspection, are discovered to be composed of white cockatoos; but their sentinel is generally too wary to let you get within shot, though you may get near enough to see them put up their yellow crests in disgust. Of sport there is not often much to be had. There may be some rabbits or some quail. On the plains there are sometimes bustards, commonly called wild turkeys, and you may get a shot at one with a rifle now and then, especially if you *drive* after them, instead of walking or riding, for they do not expect hostilities from anything on wheels. Opossums are killed by thousands for their skins, generally by hunting them up trees after dark and shooting them there. But there is no sport to be got out of them; one might as well shoot a lamb, albeit indignant with them for scampering about the roof all night. I saw a large brown one one day looking at me from a bough about ten feet off, apparently only waiting for an introduction to offer me his paw to shake. I tossed a bit of clay on to his back to make him move. He only moved a yard higher up, and taking hold with one paw of a bough of the next tree, looked down with a countenance of mild reproof, as if meekly and generously affording me the opportunity to apologize before unwillingly quitting my society.

But a station is no bed of roses for a Squatter's wife. Servants are difficult to get and to keep up the country, and especially when there are young children there is a good deal of work to be done by somebody. Then perhaps the shepherds' wives will not condescend to do any washing, and there is no one else to do it. What with hot winds, hard work, solitude and anxiety, a wife transplanted from English luxury to the bush has a hard life of it, and too soon begins to look old and worn. It is almost impossible for her to get any attention paid to the little luxuries and prettinesses of life. Perhaps the cook persists in throwing the sheep's bones into a great heap just outside the garden gate; or nobody can be spared to bury the cow that died in the home paddock, and her white skeleton has been lying there for months. To be sure, a hot wind is an effectual deodoriser, and there is only the look of the thing to be considered; but that is something, and I don't know anything that strikes a person fresh from home more than the number of carcases he sees by the roadside everywhere.

The Squatter party has been for some years powerless in the Legislature. No Squatter has much chance of being elected for the House of Assembly, and is derisively *bleated* at on the hustings if he offers himself as a candidate. Even in England I observe that a writer speaks contemptuously about their ' great ideal ' being to ' cover the continent with sheep-walks.' Surely, as regards all but a small proportion of the continent, this has been, and for some years to come will be, the ideal of every reasonable person, whether Squatter or not.

What else is to be done with the soil? Somewhere about 300,000 acres, which collected together would be equivalent in extent to a block of land a little more than twenty-one miles square, ought surely to grow enough wheat to feed the whole population of Victoria. For a quarter of wheat for each head of population, which is, I believe, the ordinary allowance in England, is probably much more than is consumed in Australia, where meat is eaten in abundance by the labouring classes. And eighteen bushels to the acre is about the average in Tasmania, where there is certainly no superabundance of capital or skill employed in farming; if Victoria cannot farm as well as that, it had better import its corn. Something must of course be added for other crops, but this amounts to comparatively little, for wheat may on most of the land be grown year after year without any rotation of crops, and with the help of subsoil ploughing without any present prospect of exhaustion. It must be remembered that meat is in England chiefly a product of agriculture, whereas in Australia it is a pastoral product. There would be no use in growing turnips or mangold (even if the climate admitted of it, which I believe it does not) in a country where there is no winter, and where stock will fatten on pasture alone. In South Australia large quantities of wheat have been grown for exportation chiefly to the other colonies, and also in one or two years to England. But in Victoria, till inland communication is very much more developed, there is no probability of its being exported to any extent; indeed I never heard of its being even suggested.

But even if this rough estimate be altogether too small, suppose that a million acres, equivalent in extent to a tract of country nearly forty miles square, or even double that quantity, were required, it would still be but a small portion of the area of Victoria. And Victoria is by far the most thickly inhabited colony. Its population is in the ratio of about seven to the square mile. As for the rest of the continent—which the Squatters are found fault with for wishing to 'cover with sheep-walks'—New South Wales contains nearly a square mile for every inhabitant, and South Australia about two and a half square miles. In England and Wales there is less than two *acres*. In speaking of the Squatters, it is only fair to remember that the colony owes its origin and existence simply and solely to them. It was they who opened up the country and made it habitable. In their hands the land, if it does not produce much, steadily improves in quality. No doubt at first they got the use of it for a merely nominal payment, but nobody else wanted it at any price, and so they paid the market value. As it become more valuable, this payment was from time to time increased. Occasionally their stations were sold, and they had the power, if they had the means, of purchasing them and becoming the absolute owners of what they had hitherto held on an uncertain tenure. If they had not the means, they had to submit to be turned out. All this was fair enough. Where land is plentiful enough, everyone should have the opportunity of purchasing it. It may be that at one time it was put up too slowly for the requirements of the growing population ; but if so, the reaction was extreme. A cry was got up and fostered for party purposes that everybody ought to be a landowner ; placards were posted along every road, stump orators vociferated, and there was a mania for getting land. From that time legislation has been unfairly directed against them. Instead of the simple plan of putting up Crown land in small blocks to the highest bidder, which in the long run would have ensured its getting into the hands of the man who would get the most out of it, elaborate Land Acts have been passed, drawn with the intention of preventing the Squatter from purchasing land at any price, even on his own run, and of parcelling his run out to different purchasers without any regard to his rights of previous occupation.

Shortly, the procedure is as follows. The district is surveyed, and blocks of a square mile each (640 acres) mapped out. Notice is given that the blocks will be put up, and numbers apply for them, the applicants hoping, if they are lucky enough to get one, to make a good bargain of it somehow, though they may not have a shilling of capital to farm it with. Amongst the rest, the Squatter on whose run the blocks are of course applies; and as amongst so many applicants his chance is small, he often increases it by engaging any one he can to make application ostensibly on his own account, but in fact as dummy for *him*, and with a view to his transfer of his interest to him should he obtain a selection. A ballot takes place on the appointed day, and the successful applicants select each his block. The Selector (or 'Cockatoo,' as he is nicknamed) thereupon obtains a seven years' lease of his 640 acres on the following terms. He is to pay a rent of one shilling per acre every half-year, in advance, to expend on improvements not less than 1*l*. per acre within three years, and to build a habitation on the land, and reside on it during his tenancy. He also covenants not to alienate. If he has fulfilled these conditions, he has the option of purchasing the freehold at the end of three years at 1*l*. per acre. If he does so, therefore, he will have expended altogether 1,472*l*., besides what his stock, &c., may have cost him.

Clearly, therefore, a Selector without any capital is practically a man 'without ostensible means of subsistence.' Yet the chance of the ballot brings many such, and how are they to live, except by stealing the Squatter's sheep and preying upon him in various petty ways? Often a Selector may be a former servant of his discharged for misconduct, who now has ample means of revenge. These additional annoyances are often worse than the original one of being deprived of large portions taken out of the midst of his best pasture. But in any case he is put to the expense of fencing in the new comer, or else letting his stock stray and feed all over the run. This alone costs about 55*l.* a mile, or 220*l.* for each selected block. And so he is often driven to throw up his run altogether, or to endeavour to evade the Act and buy out the Selector at all hazards. And the hazards are very great, for by the terms of his lease the Selector is interdicted from alienating his interest in his land, so that any bargain he may make to do so is legally void; and thus, if he happens to be a rogue, he may take the price of his block from the Squatter, and at the end of the three years refuse to give up the land to him, and snap his fingers at him. And even if the Selector who sells be an honest man and anxious to carry out the bargain fairly, the Squatter still runs a great risk; for though he can perform the requisite conditions of paying the rent and expending the 1*l.* per acre in improvements (probably a sheer waste of money to him) he cannot fulfil the other condition of residing on the block itself—for he cannot live in two or three places at once—and must trust to the forbearance of the government inspector to overlook this non-performance, otherwise the lease and the title at the end of the three years will be forfeited and his whole expenditure thrown away.

And so, as time goes on, the Squatter of moderate means is being (prematurely and needlessly, as it seems) 'civilised' off the face of Victoria. Large blocks of land have been bought up by a few of the more fortunate among them, and more often by rich merchants or speculators from the towns. Politically, as well as socially, it may well be doubted whether it is not a change for the worse. The old-fashioned Squatters were many of them sons of English gentlemen, with less wealth but with more education, knowledge of the world, and refinement, than those who are supplanting them, and they fell naturally into a position and duties in some degree resembling those of country gentlemen at home. As for the 'Cockatoos,' they have little, if anything, to be grateful for to their patrons. They have been tempted to embark in an undertaking in which three out of four have small chance of succeeding honestly. It is only in the neighbourhood of towns and markets that they are likely to do well. Already, though the last Act has hardly been three years in operation, a deputation of them has been to the government, declaring their inability to pay their purchase-money and petitioning for an abatement.

I am very far from pretending to possess a complete knowledge and understanding of the land-questions and the land-laws in Victoria. But the present system seems so patently and obviously bad that he who runs may read that it is so. The possibility of obtaining land by the chance of the ballot is unsettling and demoralising, just as in a greater degree a public lottery is. Its tendency is to hand over the soil, not to skilled and thrifty agriculturists, but to speculators or to idle men who have failed at other trades, and who try their luck at the ballot on the chance of making a good bargain somehow or other if they draw a lucky number. The blocks are so large, require so much capital, and are often at such a distance from a market, that they are quite unsuitable for a peasant agriculturist, who can seldom obtain any labour but his own and that of his children. The discretionary power, which in certain cases is vested in the Executive, of selling or not selling land on particular runs, gives it an immense and undue influence, and is liable to lead, as experience has shown, to gross corruption amongst members of the Assembly and others who have influence with the Ministers for the time being. Eventually the system will, it is believed, after great waste of labour, and after ruining a number of Squatters, throw the land into the hands of the monster capitalists far more certainly than if a much less extent, favourably situated, had been put up to auction in much smaller blocks. In the meantime, the class of agriculturists, or quasi-agriculturists, has been artificially increased so as to be out of proportion to the rest of the population. And as one political fault, unrepented of, soon necessitates another, a protective duty on corn has been imposed, which helps, as far as it goes, to prop up the land laws.

But neither Protection nor an artificial land system will do the agriculturists much good in the end, not even if a clause could be introduced and enforced obliging everybody to eat two quarters of wheat a year instead of one. A few good big ships full of immigrants do more for them than all the land laws in the world. For what they want is more mouths for them to feed. And in the long run new mouths will go most to countries where, *cæteris paribus,* industry and labour are left, not only unfettered but unpampered, to find their own level in their own way.

The present land laws savour of unjust class legislation, of tyranny of the majority over the minority. Yet so little confidence is placed in the present Legislative Assembly, that it is expected that any change which may be made will be for the worse. Democracy has made a bad beginning in Australia. At this rate, what with bad legislation and the far worse and more fatal vice of corruption, it will be well if the word 'democracy' does not in course of time earn for itself in this part of the world a *special* sense as derogatory as that which the word 'tyranny' did in Greece of old.

## V.

### POLITICS IN VICTORIA.

Strange to say, it is a fact notorious in Victoria that a proportion of the Legislative Assembly, sufficient to sway its vote on almost any measure that may be introduced, is altogether corrupt and amenable to bribes! How long this has been so I know not, or how long it has been a matter of notoriety; but attention has been particularly drawn in this direction lately by the scandalous disclosures made in the case of *Sands* v. *Armstrong,* which was tried in May. The plaintiff was a member of the Assembly, against whom charges were made in a local paper of so serious a nature that he was compelled to bring an action for libel, to endeavour to re-establish his character. The trial lasted several days, and resulted in a verdict of a farthing damages—practically, of course, a verdict for the defendant—as nearly all the charges against the plaintiff were fully made out. The following extracts from a leading article in the *Argus* of May 6, 1867, describe his operations:—

> For years past there has been a prevalent belief that rank jobbery and corruption infested our governing system, and from time to time circumstances came to light which confirmed and

strengthened this belief. But outside political circles the facts were not known with certainty, while as to the extent of the evil the general public could not even form a guess. At last we have got at the truth, so far as concerns the operations of one honourable member. For the first time the veil has been completely lifted, and the life of a jobbing legislator fully exposed to view. And the reality is immeasurably worse than any but the initiated could have imagined. Scheme and trick and dodge are proved to have been the constant practice of the person whose conduct has been investigated, his public position a mere agency by which he could work out, by means of wholesale corruption, sordid plans of personal aggrandizement. . . . . . Using his influence with the Government, and pretending to greater influence than we are willing to believe they ever permitted him to exercise, he seems to have meddled in every kind of public business transacted in his locality, and turned it to account for his own pecuniary gain. Nothing was above—nothing beneath him. If a poor labouring man wanted a bit of land under the 42nd Clause, it was ten shillings to Sands; if there was a returning officer to be appointed, that was an affair of 30*l*. if it could be managed. Circumstances rendered one piece of local preferment particularly desirable during the currency of his operations, by reason of its great profitableness, and that he apparently tried to keep in his own hands altogether, appointing a dummy official representative (though on this part of the case the evidence is necessarily incomplete, the only persons fully cognizant of the facts having been accomplices in the transaction). But there is no doubt of his having professed to be able to influence the administration of the law. . . . . . . Is the Attorney-General to be worked by such as Sands? No one will for a moment believe so; but his claiming to possess such influence shows how hardened he had become through long immunity from exposure and punishment. . . . He has a newspaper, and he has also a public-house, both of which seem to have served as tolls for the collection of corruption-money. But in aid of these he established an agency far more efficient than either. This was in the form of a testimonial to himself, and the subscription lists being kept open for a year and a half were a constant appeal to the generosity of all who had anything to gain from the favour of the Government or to fear from its displeasure.

If the case of Sands had been a solitary and exceptional one, it would not have called for remark. But his course of conduct seems to have been singular chiefly in having been found out. Opinions differ slightly as to the number of Members, who, if not quite as bad as Sands, nevertheless lay themselves out for bribes outside the House, and are ready to sell their votes in the House for a sufficient consideration. The *Argus* (if I recollect right) reckons about ten or twelve. But nobody, except a Member or two in a parliamentary and perfunctory way in the House, seriously attempts to deny the existence of such a set, most of whom are as notorious as if they occupied a special bench to themselves. Nevertheless, I was surprised to hear a well informed and moderate man, not specially connected with politics, express his opinion that almost any measure might be carried through the House for the sum of 15,000*l.* judiciously expended in bribes. I repeated this with some hesitation, lest he should be sensitive to such a reflection on his colleagues, to a Member. He answered by coolly counting up the purchasable Members on his fingers, and concluded that it could be done for a less sum, remarking that a clever, unscrupulous man, possessing great wealth and popular manners, might obtain almost unlimited power in the Assembly. Nor is the blame of this disgraceful state of things to be laid specially to the charge of the present Ministry. They have indeed been content to let things go on in the old groove, and in the matter of the Sands scandal have not appeared very anxious to promote an investigation. But their personal integrity, and, on the whole, their ability, is well spoken of by men of all parties. Even the Opposition, opposed as it is to their ultra-democratic and protectionist policy, confess that their places could not well be supplied, should they have to quit office, and that a change is more likely to be for the worse than for the better.

Jobbing in Government patronage is one source of corruption. Under the O'Shanassy Government (in some respects considered to have been one of the best) it is said to have been almost impossible for any but Irish and Roman Catholics to obtain any place. Even the porters on the railways completed at that time are Irish almost to a man. But this is comparatively a small matter. It is the Lands Office which is the focus of corruption, and it is the unsettled state of the land laws and regulations which affords such opportunities for roguery. For instance, under a clause of the Land Act of 1865, any person residing near the gold-fields may, subject to the sanction of the Lands Office, select and purchase, at a fixed price, any portion of Crown land within a certain distance, not exceeding a certain quantity. This clause the Minister of Lands has seen fit to extend to Crown lands (which are in general Squatters' runs) at any distance from the gold-fields—in fact, almost anywhere. Other clauses leave a somewhat similar discretion with the Minister. Thus, he continually has in his own hands the power of selling or refusing to sell Crown land, and practically he generally gives or withholds his sanction in each instance according to the recommendation of the Member for the district, or, if this Member happens not to be a supporter of the Government, of some other who is. Thus, a Squatter may sometimes be deprived of a block of land in the middle of his run, if he prove troublesome to a Government candidate. It is unnecessary to point out what a temptation this offers to a needy Member, and how it almost forces the Squatter to illegal practices for his own protection. I once heard a Squatter, an honourable and much respected man, say that, wanting to purchase a part of his own run which was Crown land, he had sent orders to a land agent at Melbourne to apply for it for him, and that his instructions were to obtain it, if possible without, but if not possible by, the help of *parliamentary influence.* I innocently asked him what parliamentary influence meant. He answered simply that it meant a fee of 5*l.* to one or more members to urge and support the application.

People seem to resign themselves to the existence of a corrupt House of Assembly as to a necessary evil, a thing inevitable. I have heard the free-trade party blamed for not *buying,* as it is said they easily might have done, sufficient support to enable them to establish their policy. Such an opinion sounds horrible enough in the mouth of an honourable man. It reminds one of the purchase of the Irish Parliament in 1800, which few will say was not necessary to be done, and which was done by honest men, though it would puzzle a casuist to justify it. The judge who tried the case of *Sands* v. *Armstrong*, in his summing-up declared that the evidence had made him a convert to the proposal of payment of Members, for that, as they gained no credit or social distinction by their membership, they expected a pecuniary consideration for their trouble, and it was better for them to get it honestly and above-board than dishonestly. The House, it seems, thinks so too, for by a majority of 22 to 10, the other day, they patriotically voted that they ought to be paid. The Council will probably throw out the Bill, for it may be doubted whether a moderate salary would suffice to induce a rogue even to confine his rogueries within the bounds of decency.

These things being so in Victoria, and being no secret, but in every man's mouth, it is not a little humiliating to find the peculiar institutions under which such abuses thrive, held up, in a volume of *Essays on Reform*, apparently as a pattern by which England may profit in remodelling her own. I have neither space nor inclination to examine the essay in detail. The account which it gives of Australian prosperity is, no doubt, true enough. Indeed, as regards Victoria, nobody need be otherwise than sanguine about the ultimate prospects of a colony of such extraordinary natural wealth. It will require very bad legislation, and a very bad legislature indeed, to inflict any irretrievable blow on its material prosperity. The Council is as yet sound, and works well. Above all, the Bench is excellently filled. It is true that there are many unrefined and wholly uneducated persons in the wealthiest class; the largest proprietor (in fee) of land in Australia, and probably in the world, was once a retail butcher. But this will right itself by degrees. And, on the other hand, the lowest class in Victoria is decidedly superior in energy and intelligence to the same class in England, as is to be expected of the first generation of colonists who have come out each of his own individual will, and not forced in a promiscuous mass by any political convulsion. It is a pleasure to see a man breaking stones on the road, he does it with such vigour, and one knows he is earning thereby about five shillings a day, and not only a pittance at the workhouse. Victorian society is like English, with a thick slice cut off the top and a thin slice off the bottom. There is, perhaps, more to be said for universal suffrage in Victoria than in most countries.

But admitting all this, the utmost that the writer of this essay has proved by it is that these colonies have not been retarded in their growth by their peculiar institutions. He does indeed contrast the excellent judges of the present time with a drunken Judge-Advocate under Governor Bligh. But in those days New South Wales had scarcely ceased to be anything more than a huge prison, and he might as well compare a judge of the Court of Queen's Bench to an Old Bailey practitioner. The press of the present time, no doubt, is superior to that of fifteen or twenty years ago. So is the press of London to that of Birmingham or Dublin; but is that because London has a better political constitution than they have, or because it has many times their population, and is able to demand and pay for better and more expensively conducted publications? As to public expenditure, it is idle to compare old and burdened countries with new ones in this respect, but is it so great a triumph for a Legislature which entered upon its labours with no debt, no foreign ministers, no pauperism, almost no military or naval expenses, no possibility of war, a population extraordinarily wealthy, and millions of acres of land to sell when it pleased, not to have exceeded its income (though in Victoria the Government has fallen back on Protection for revenue), while England, with more than a third of her revenue going to pay interest of debt, with the pauperism of an overcrowded country, and with foreign war constantly threatening, has yet managed, however little, to continue paying off her debt?

Nobody disputes the desirability of representative institutions for colonies which have reached a certain stage of development. The point is whether they have worked the better in Australia for being so democratic, and this the essay scarcely even attempts to prove. Still less does it prove that such institutions, even if they are the best it was practicable to obtain for Australia, would be equally applicable under utterly different circumstances in England. With respect to the glaring evils I have alluded to, the writer may perhaps agree with the author of another essay in the same volume, that corruption in the Legislature is, 'except in extreme cases,' merely 'an annoying and offensive, and not a dangerous disease.' This is the old cry of 'measures, not men,' revived. For my own part, I believe that the tardiest and feeblest legislation is far less pregnant with fatal consequences than the habitual contemplation of dishonesty in high places and amongst public men. This is an ever-present pattern and incentive to evil, which, entering every household, offers its drop of poison to every ambitious and aspiring man, and slowly and imperceptibly brings all that is sterling and honourable into disrepute.

## VI.

### TASMANIA.

THE heat, and drought, and dust of summer begin to make Melbourne unpleasant by December. In Sydney and Adelaide it is hotter still, and in Queensland there is almost as great heat as in India, without all the elaborate Indian appliances and luxuries for making it bearable. Christmas holidays and lawyers' Long Vacation are just beginning. Hence there is a considerable migration about this time of year of Australians on the mainland who may be ailing or wanting a holiday, to the cool fresh air of Tasmania; and well filled steamers go about twice a week from Melbourne to either Launceston or Hobart Town, and once a fortnight from Sydney.

Our long narrow vessel, crowded with passengers and incommoded with an unpleasant deck-cargo of two or three hundred sheep, which makes her roll like a porpoise, steams swiftly away from Melbourne down the dirty sluggish Yarra-Yarra, between flat marshy banks, more malodoriferous than the worst parts of the Thames in its worst days. By sunset we are out of Port Phillip and in Bass's Straits. Next morning we pass high jagged rocky islands, rising abruptly and precipitously out of deep water; then through Banks's Straits, which seem to be a funnel for collecting the wind, for it is almost always blowing hard there from the west; and in the afternoon we glide suddenly out of the rough water into the serenest and calmest of seas, protected from the fierce westerly winds by Tasmania, the east coast of which lies a few miles off to starboard, a pretty peaceful shelving shore, with bold mountains rising up in the distance. Another night at sea, and we wake up at daylight as the vessel is rounding the fine precipitous headlands of Cape Pillar and Cape Raoul, with basaltic columns like those in the cliffs of the Giant's Causeway, and is entering Storm Bay with its wooded islands, narrow-necked peninsulas, and deep inlets running far into the country, till the eye is puzzled to discern where our course will be, and to distinguish island from coast. Two hours more and the estuary of the Derwent is reached, broad, but as we proceed wholly land-locked by hilly shores, rising gently from the water's edge, and green with cultivation near their base, their summits dark with trees and half-cleared bush. I can think of nothing to compare it with unless it be the Lake of Thun without its snow mountains, or the Dart at its widest near Dartmouth; but both are bad comparisons. Soon after, the dark blue-grey wooded mass of Mount Wellington faces us, rising up four thousand feet and more; and on the sloping shores of the little bay below it lies Hobart Town, with wharves along the water's edge, and water deep enough for a man-of-war within two hundred yards of the shore. Sea, river, mountain, forest, farm, and city, are before the eye almost at once. It is the most beautiful spot for a city I ever saw in the world.

The steamer comes alongside a deserted looking wharf, occupied only by two or three drays and carriages, and a knot or two of lounging, ill-conditioned porters; and with the picture of busy, thriving, restless, eager Melbourne fresh upon our minds, we land, to find ourselves in what looks like a pleasant, neat, old-fashioned English country town, perhaps twice as large and straggling as Dorchester, Ipswich, or Bury, but ten times more stagnant, dull, and lifeless. A greater contrast in every way to Melbourne could hardly be conceived. At Melbourne most people seem to be there only for business, that they may accumulate and save money and retire with it to England. Of Hobart Town the most conspicuous and characteristic feature is the number of small, quiet, comfortable houses in small, pretty, gay gardens, such as men with incomes of from 300*l.* to 800*l.* might inhabit, and which look like the abodes of retired sea-captains, merchants, or tradesmen. The House of Assembly and Custom-house, the Post-office, and other public offices, are very well placed in a central position not far from the wharves—handsome, stone-faced, neatly-finished buildings, free from attempts at florid ornamentation, and though small and unpretending, more appropriate, and in better taste, than many of the public buildings of

Melbourne or Sydney. They were planned and begun, most of them, in the days when there was any amount of convict labour available, and have been finished since, at heavy cost owing to the dearness of labour, by the help of loans, the interest of which presses somewhat heavily on the colony. But so seldom is anyone to be seen passing in or out of them, that one doubts at first sight whether they can be in use.

The streets are almost empty. Nobody looks busy. Nobody is in a hurry. Converse with anyone about the state of the Colony, and the word *depression* is one of the first you hear, and it will come over and over again till you are weary of it. Different people mean different things by it, and feel the tendency from prosperity to adversity in different ways, but few or none dispute the fact. Elderly ladies lament the old days when there was more society, and a more abundant supply of soldier and sailor ball-partners; merchants and tradesmen the time when Hobart Town promised to be the emporium if not the metropolis of Australia. It is seldom indeed that anyone can be heard to speak cheerily of the present, or hopefully of the future of Tasmania. Nor is the colony suffering merely from one of those temporary checks in the advance of prosperity, which always occur from time to time in young colonies,—such as, for instance, the wide-spread ruin in Queensland, which was mainly, and so strangely, caused by the commercial panic in London, and which is already passing away. Tasmania (or Van Diemen's Land, as it was originally called—the name was changed to efface, if possible, the very memory of its identity and existence as a convict colony) is the oldest next to New South Wales of the Australian colonies, and till twenty or twenty-five years ago was still, next to it, the most important. Now it is thrown completely into the shade by Victoria, South Australia, and even by Queensland. For the last fifteen years the revenue, the trade, the shipping, and the general prosperity and enterprise of the colony have been steadily decreasing. And although the population has increased, the increase has been due solely to the excess of births over deaths, and not at all to immigration— the number of persons who have left the colony during this period being considerably in excess of those who have arrived in it, in spite of very large sums spent out of the public money on immigration—and hence the population of adults has remained nearly stationary, while only that of old people and children has increased. A settler of twenty or thirty years' standing, especially in the southern part of the island, can perhaps point to only one or two houses in his township which have been built since he came.

It is not difficult to account for this state of things. Wool first, and then gold have been the two principal causes of prosperity in Australia. Of gold there is not sufficient quantity in Tasmania to pay for working it. Wool it does produce according to its capabilities; but it must not be forgotten that the island is comparatively small (roughly, about as big as Ireland), that much of it is thickly timbered or for other reasons useless, and only a small proportion available for pasture. What there is has been almost all taken up and made the most of, for nearly thirty years past. And so mere excess of numbers drove men, and young men especially, away from Tasmania, to become Squatters in Victoria, and in younger colonies where there was more room for them. For the most profitable sheep-farming, according to the present system and condition of things, is that which is done on a large scale. Ten thousand acres is a very small station. I have heard of as much as seven hundred thousand acres, the size of a large English county, belonging to one cattle-station in a remote part of Queensland. It is said that sixty thousand sheep is about the best and most economical number for a Squatter to have, that being large enough and not too large for him to manage, with the assistance of his overseer and shepherds. And sixty thousand sheep take a great many acres of the thin thirsty Australian grass to keep them alive through the summer droughts.

It is true that Tasmania with its excellent and temperate climate is especially suitable for agriculture. According to the government statistics the average produce of an acre of wheat is about eighteen bushels. In England the average is said to be twenty-eight, in Ireland twenty-four, and in France only fifteen and a half.* And bearing in mind that in a new country the cheapness of land and dearness of labour and of capital renders farming almost of necessity slovenly, this may

* *Our Daily Food.* By James Caird.

be considered a comparatively large yield. But there are great difficulties in the way of the agriculturist. Most of the rich chocolate-coloured soil in the north is very heavily timbered, and requires much labour to clear it. It is seldom indeed that farming is made remunerative, even by settlers who have had many years' experience, except in the immediate neighbourhood of a large town. For it must be remembered that the population of an Australian colony is very small, comparatively, and its market soon glutted; and that as the town and manufacturing population is small compared with the country population, the tendency is always in the long run rather towards over supply of agricultural produce, and consequent low prices. Now and then of course there is a violent reaction; but the great fluctuation in price is of itself an evil and a difficulty. The crop that pays best one year may, however abundant, be a loss the next.* A farmer needs something of the judgment and experience of a merchant and of a speculator to enable him to succeed, as well as skill to grow good crops. And often capital is thrown away upon a soil which is too poor to repay cultivation; for it is difficult to form a correct opinion of the value of land which has never been cultivated. One often passes fields which have been abandoned, and in one place I saw a whole valley left to return into its original condition of bush.

* As an instance of this it may be mentioned that cheese, which in March 1868 was selling at fourteenpence a pound, was in December of the same year selling at fivepence halfpenny.

Tasmania has suffered, too, more perhaps than even New South Wales, though in a way that is less likely to be permanent, from the abuse of the convict system. I say the *abuse* of it, for looking upon transportation to Australia as a whole, I find it impossible to avoid the conclusion that it has been a great and conspicuous success. But poor Tasmania was very hardly treated. In 1840—rashly and needlessly as Lord Grey thought *—transportation to New South Wales was suddenly stopped, and the whole stream turned on the unfortunate island. For many years after this the convicts far outnumbered the free population. In 1845 there were 25,000 male convicts in the island, and the country was simply a huge penal settlement without even sufficient room for expansion, the moral sink and sewer of England. It is true that in this colony the convicts were seldom able to marry or leave children, or settle on the land, as they did in New South Wales, and that the great majority left the country as soon as their sentences expired, so that considering the immense number brought there, the number now remaining is surprisingly small. It may also be true, as is asserted (though I hardly believe it), that crime measured by the number of convictions is now not more frequent than in England, in proportion to the population. Still in one way or another they have left a curse behind them. The settlers were demoralized by the assignment system, which while it lasted gave them almost

---

* *Colonial Policy of Lord J. Russell*, vol. ii. p. 4.

the power of slave-holders. A convict could be hired for little more than the cost of maintaining him; sometimes in consideration of leisure allowed him, he even paid money to his master in addition to his services; and the master could get him even punished at the public expense by sending him to the nearest magistrate with the written message, 'Please give the bearer twenty lashes, and return him to yours truly.'

Free labour, as is always the case, suffered from contact with forced labour. The convict taught the free labourer many bad lessons, and one of them was how to do the least possible amount of work for a day's wages. The accepted standard of a day's work became a low one. Wages might fall, but such labour was dear at any price. All this time the Home Government was spending about half a million annually in the colony, and was making roads, harbours, and wharves, on a magnificent scale by convict labour; so that the cost was not felt in taxation. Government originated everything, planned everything, paid for everything. An unhealthy artificial condition of society was produced which tended to enervate all classes, and left the colony ill prepared to stand against, or profit by, the events which followed. In deference to the general outcry at its gross abuse, transportation was suddenly stopped, and with it ceased most of the annual half million from England. At this time Victoria had for some years past been attracting from Tasmania many of the most enterprising and adventurous of its population, but from the moment when the wonderful news of the gold came, it seemed as if none would be left behind but old men, women, and children. Most would indeed have done better to stay behind and cultivate the land. For wheat rose till it sold for five to six pounds a quarter in Melbourne, and hay at from twenty to forty pounds a ton. A great trade sprang up with Melbourne in corn, timber, vegetables, and fruit, and there was a hope that Tasmania would establish itself as the granary of Victoria. But year by year this trade has been diminishing, and now American flour and even American timber undersell Tasmanian in the Melbourne market. Some fortunes indeed were made in those years of gold, but they were comparatively few and small, and those who made them have for the most part invested them elsewhere, or been content to live quietly on the interest of the money rather than risk their capital in doubtful enterprises.

For there more than elsewhere in Australia—as much, perhaps, take the whole year round, as anywhere in the world—do scenery and climate invite retirement to country life. It is the Capua of the Australias. Snow scarcely falls except to ornament the summits of Mount Wellington and of the distant ranges of the uninhabited and almost unexplored west coast. The frosts are seldom fatal even to the tenderest plant. The stifling hot winds of the continent are cooled by a hundred miles of sea before they reach the island. Nor is the air stagnant or sultry. Hot as the sun is by day, the summer nights are cooler than in England. English trees, flowers, and fruits, flourish with a rare luxuriance, side by side with pines from Norfolk Island and New Zealand. Geraniums blaze out in huge pink and scarlet masses, growing in almost wild profusion. The English sweet-briar has been introduced, and has spread of itself till in its luxuriance it has become a noxious weed to the farmers. Fruit follows fruit so fast under the early summer sun that apples ripen almost before strawberries are over. It is in such profusion that it lies rotting on the ground for want of mouths to eat it. Life is long here, and you seldom see the pale, thin, dried-up, prematurely old faces and lean figures of the other colonies, which almost make one doubt whether the English race was meant to live in climates such as those of Queensland and of South Australia. Sometimes indeed it seems as if the climate were *too* Capuan, too little compelling to exertion. Invalids bask in it, rheumatic people find in it relief from pain, and the consumptive live out the full tale of their days. But the strong and active seem to lose something of their vigour, to ride where they used to walk, to walk where they used to run, to drink stimulants when they used to eat. Children seem to grow up less hardy for want of the nipping of the keen frost and the bitter blast of the English east wind to compel them to activity and to make repose for half the year, except by the fire-side, impossible.*

* I regret to say that accounts lately received (February 1869) represent the depressed state of the colony as worse than ever, the prospects of the coming harvest, owing to continued drought, being in some districts very bad. It is with still greater regret that I learn that there is a popular outcry for constructing a rail-

way across the island from Hobart Town to Launceston, which it is supposed will be a panacea for all depression and stagnation of trade. That the short railway now in course of construction from Launceston to the western districts will bring advantages adequate to the outlay, even though it may not pay a profit in itself, there is every reason to hope, for it will open communication with a magnificent new agricultural district. But the country between Hobart Town and Launceston is in general not specially fertile; it has for many years past been traversed by an exceptionally excellent road, over which one daily coach each way is for the greater part of the year more than sufficient for the passenger traffic. There is no prospect of any considerable interchange of commodities between the two towns, as each is sufficiently supplied with food from its own district, and each has a harbour for the introduction of imports and shipping of exports. The distance is about 120 miles, with much difference of level and consequent engineering difficulties. The loans and taxation necessary for its construction will be a grievous additional burden on the colony, which it is very ill able to bear. These considerations are so obvious to every one that the popularity of the scheme must be attributed in a great measure to sheer recklessness on the part of many of those who advocate it—and indeed it is said that this has been in some quarters admitted. The money borrowed in England will doubtless improve trade for a year or two till it is all spent, and what follows is to be left to the chapter of accidents. Great and praiseworthy efforts have been made by the present administration to pare down the expenditure of the colony to a level with the revenue—which it was considered impossible to increase by additional taxation—and it is to be hoped they will not embark without due consideration on so dangerous a scheme, and imperil the credit of the colony which they have done so much to sustain.

## VII.

### TASMANIA (*continued*).

CIRCUMSTANCES have made Tasmania lean more than any other of the Australian Colonies towards sober conservatism in its ideas and its social and political aspect. Perhaps the youthful ideal of those who are now middle-aged and influential was generally the British regimental officer, as he was to be found, some twenty or thirty years ago, in quarters at Hobart Town, or retired and occupied with his grant of land up the country. For in those days there were sometimes a couple of regiments in the colony, which formed no unimportant or inconsiderable proportion of its population, besides a number of government officials in various capacities. The original landed proprietors were mostly retired officers of the army or navy, army doctors, or other government officials, to whom up to about thirty-five years ago grants of land were made by the Crown.

Land was not worth very much then. Ploughing your field with a sentry keeping guard at one end of it lest you should be speared by a black fellow crawling out of the bush, was farming under difficulties: to say nothing of the probability of having the station cleared out by bushrangers from time to time, and the chance of being shot, as a precaution against identification, by men who had already forfeited their lives.

It is better than any novel to get an old Tasmanian settler to tell you about those old times, the uproarious, dare-devil, killing and robbing heroic age of the colony. The crowning event, the great joke of the time—soon after which things began to get comparatively peaceable and prosaic—was the 'black war,' as it is ironically called. This was one of the wildest and most impracticable schemes ever devised by a really wise man, for catching the black fellows alive and unhurt and deporting them to some island where they might be both harmless and safe. All available soldiers and settlers were mustered and posted in a continuous line across the south-eastern corner of the country, which line, advancing day by day and gradually converging, was at length to enclose and catch them as in a trap. It was like sending half a dozen mastiffs to drive rabbits out of a wood, as almost every one knew beforehand it would be. Somebody caught (I think) one black man and a woman, very much by accident, and no more were even *seen*. But 30,000*l.* or 40,000*l.* had been spent on the campaign, and when the campaigners sent the bill home accompanied by a memorial setting out magniloquently the glorious results attained, John Bull unsuspectingly paid it, and the colony was so much the richer for its 'black war.'

Very soon after this—but in no sort of way in consequence of it—the whole race of aborigines came one by one and voluntarily gave themselves up to a man named Robinson, who had acquired an extraordinary influence over them, and who deserves to be nominated patron saint of the colony. They were settled on Flinders Island and kindly treated, but nevertheless died off fast. The small remnant was afterwards settled at Oyster Cove, an exquisitely lovely spot on D'Entrecasteaux' Channel, where the survivors, now only three in number, are to be seen.

The bushrangers too were put down soon after the black fellows had been removed; and though others appeared from time to time, they could never escape capture very long, not having, as escaped convicts had in New South Wales, any sympathisers among the settlers; and now for many years past no such thing as a bushranger has been heard of in Tasmania.

As the country became safe, land became valuable, and was sold instead of being granted away, and sheep and wool brought a certain degree of prosperity. Still no great amount of wealth was made by the settlers up the country, and in the towns those who made money by trade generally migrated with it to Victoria, and settled there where there was more scope for them, and the less adventurous built themselves comfortable houses in or immediately around Hobart Town; so that the original landowners have not been supplanted so much as might have been expected, considering the events and changes which have taken place, by rich mercantile men or tradesmen; but in the bad times of late years have either disappeared altogether, leaving their places vacant, or continue on the same property, seldom richer, and often much poorer, than when they were younger. In the list of magistrates there are still * fifteen who were on the commission before 1835.

Very many persons have not once left the island since they came to settle in it, or were born in it. It is quite a new sensation to live amongst people, comparatively few of whom, rich or poor, old or young, have ever seen a railway. The old came before railways were made anywhere, and both live in a country where a Bill to make the first has only this week passed the Legislature.

Nevertheless, with all their conservatism, during the ten years since the first Parliament under the new Constitution met, the Government has been changed seven times, four Parliaments have been elected, and only three Members of the House of Assembly have kept their seats during the whole time. The latter contains a considerable 'rowdy' element, which has introduced a degree of scurrilousness and coarse personal abuse, astonishing to decorous English ears, into hustings speeches and occasionally into parliamentary debates. On one occasion, the Head of the Government, when received with disfavour by the Assembly, appealed from it for sympathy to the spectators. Shortly afterwards, when he had left office, he was, for gross misconduct, expelled by a vote of the House from sitting there for a year. Yet he is still a prominent

* January 1867.

member of the Opposition, and is one of the three Members who have been returned for every Parliament.

The administration ordinarily consists of a colonial secretary, a treasurer, and an attorney-general, one of whom is Premier. The duties of office are not so onerous as to prevent a minister pursuing his ordinary avocations, such as those of barrister or merchant.

The legislative power is vested, as in all the Australian colonies which have a constitution, in two Houses, corresponding to our Lords and Commons, and actually using May's *Parliamentary Practice* as their text-book on points of order. The upper House or Legislative Council of Tasmania contains fifteen members, each of whom sits for six years from the date of his election. This House is not subject to dissolution by the Governor. Its members are chosen by electoral districts, the electors being freeholders to the amount of 50*l.* a year, doctors, ministers of religion, graduates of a university, barristers, and army or navy officers, resident twelve months prior to the election. The Lower House, or Legislative Assembly, is chosen by ten-pound householders, and is subject to dissolution by the Governor, who now has much the same powers in the colony that the Crown has in England.

This ten-pound franchise is in the towns practically equivalent to household suffrage. In the country the labourers in general have no votes, as they live rent-free in houses belonging to their employers. No lowering of the franchise has ever been seriously demanded or proposed, and indeed there has been hardly any such thing as a genuine democratic cry; but from time to time sham 'poor man's friend' cries are got up for election purposes. Those who get them up are so notoriously worthless, that most honest people here are inspired with contempt for democratic cries and democrats everywhere, and when they read their English news have less toleration for noisy demagogues than an average English Tory would have. Yet here, as in England, such opinions are oftener expressed in private than in public, and there is apparently the same shrinking from plain outspoken denunciation of the evils of an unmixed democracy—evils the approach of which so true a lover of liberty as De Tocqueville constantly deplored, as certain to be, sooner or later, fatal to both freedom and patriotism.

Intimidation of voters is out of the question in a country where there are scarcely any large employers of labour, and where the relation of landlord is comparatively rare, has none of the traditions of feudalism in it, and is subject to no obligation but that of money payment. In general a seat in the House of Assembly is not so much coveted as to have any money value, so that there is no inducement to bribery. The only constituency, I was told, amongst which it has been practised is that of Hobart Town itself. In this, the only instance in which the ballot could have been of use, it (on one occasion at least) signally failed. An ingenious method was practised of evading its secresy, and making it certain that the bribees carried out their contract. The system of voting was for each voter to be presented, on entering the polling-booth, with a voting-paper, duly signed, containing the names of *both* the candidates. This the voter took into the room containing the ballot-box, where he erased the name for which he did *not* wish to vote, and then deposited it in the box. The trick was done as follows: Bribee number one was instructed to pass through without depositing his voting-paper at all, but to give it after he came out to the bribing agent. The agent then erased from it the hostile candidate's name, and gave it to bribee number two, who deposited it in the ballot-box, bringing out his *own* paper entire, which, after the Opposition name had been erased, was in like manner handed to bribee number three, and so on, the bribees having thus no opportunity of voting wrong without being discovered.

In conversation members not only of the Legislature but of the Ministry do not hesitate to avow their conviction that the granting of the new Constitution has proved to be a mistake and a misfortune to the country, and that the old one worked better, under which ministers held office permanently and a proportion of members of the Assembly were nominated by the Governor. It is not that the government, as compared with that of the neighbouring colonies, has not on the whole been well carried on. Under the discouraging circumstances of a steadily diminishing revenue, which had to be met from time to time by increased taxation, the public debt amounts to 5*l*. 10*s*. per head as against 13*l*. 17*s*. 6*d* in prosperous Victoria; and the taxation to 2*l.* 11*s.* per head annually against 4*l.* 12*s.* 4*d.* in Victoria. The men of education and respectability have in general succeeded in maintaining an ascendency over the unprincipled and rowdy element, though the latter is always at least a strong minority. But there is something unsuitable and almost comical in adapting the ponderous machinery of *quasi* Crown, Lords, and Commons to so small a community. A popular House requires numbers to give it any appearance of importance, and it is impossible that there can be very much dignity in a very miscellaneous assembly, containing when all are present only thirty members; although a reasonable proportion of them are men of fair average ability, and there is nothing of pomposity or self-importance in the demeanour of the speakers. Strangers are admitted into the body of the House, and sit on benches or on the floor all about the Speaker's chair, and though this arrangement is rather disorderly, it is perhaps an assistance to the speakers to have their small audience a little increased.

The title of *Honourable* has been accorded to members of the upper House; but so conscious are they, apparently, of its inappropriateness, that in assuming it they do not drop the title of esquire, and Mr. Smith of the Legislative Council is the Honourable John Smith, Esquire.

And there is a very practical, and not merely æsthetic, inappropriateness and inconvenience in too soon conferring almost complete independence, and consequent isolation, on a small community. It is true the mere possession of a sufficient amount of territory rightly gives importance and a position of dignity in the world. Tasmania being about the size of Ireland, and geographically very well situated, is quite *big* enough to stand almost alone. But its entire population, town and country, is under a hundred thousand, less than that of a moderately large manufacturing town in the old world. Making it self-governing tends to cut off the supply from home of educated men who used to go out in various official positions. As a new generation grows up, its ranks are no longer increased by those who have had a more complete education and a wider experience in the old world. By most of the older generation of colonists this isolation is felt and deplored as an evil. But the younger ones cannot be expected to look upon the matter in the same light; and as an instance of this, an attempt was lately made to abolish two scholarships which are annually given out of the public money by competitive examination for sending and maintaining two students at an English University. The Bill passed the lower House almost without opposition, and the scholarships were only saved in the upper House by a narrow majority obtained by the strenuous protest of one of its Members.

Interest in the details of imperial questions of necessity grows weaker year by year. It is not that loyalty to the old country and to the crown is decaying. None would repudiate such an idea more than the Tasmanians. Their Tasmanianism is to them scarcely more than an accident, which the fact of their being English far transcends in importance. Considering its age, this colony retains a more completely English character than any of the others. But the rising generation knows England only by tradition and by books. And of the older men throughout Australia many feel somewhat keenly the indifference shown to the colonies by England.

Those in particular who by tradition or by the natural bent of their minds are conservative, have, in fighting their hopeless battle against the excesses of democracy, looked almost in vain during the last fifteen years for support or sympathy to the political party in England from whom they had a right to expect it. Such neglect could not fail to alienate their interest in English politics. And when the news came that the cause of their old party at home was not only lost, but its political honour indelibly stained by the unprincipled and time-serving policy of its leaders, it seemed like a last act of painful severance from their old hopes and traditions of political life.

The parliament of a colony, especially one so small in population as Tasmania, can have in general only petty local questions to discuss. With no foreign relations, such as an altogether independent state has, and therefore no foreign policy, and generally with no clearly defined or special domestic policy either, there are no opposing principles for opposite parties to adopt. The result is that, so far from agreeing, they divide with tenfold greater hostility and rancour on personal and private grounds. It is sometimes difficult, when a government is defeated and resigns, for the Governor to know whom to send for to form a new Ministry. The plan at first resorted to, of sending for the proposer of the hostile motion, might not improbably result in obtaining a new Premier with no other claim or qualification for the office than his hostility to his predecessor.

An instance of personal and party feeling overriding plain public justice occurred some years ago, in the case of one of the judges—with this one exception always a good set—who endeavoured to borrow money of a suitor pending the decision on his case. The suitor refused and made the scandal known; whereupon the judge, fearing the consequences, pleaded ill-health and applied for a retiring ill-health pension in the ordinary way. This the government, under the circumstances, refused; but afterwards, finding that the judge would not voluntarily resign without a pension, and that his partisans and friends in the House were too strong to allow a vote of the House summarily dismissing him to pass, they were compelled to bring in and pass a special Act granting him the full amount of the pension asked for, as the only means of getting rid of him from the bench. Shortly afterwards, his alleged bad health notwithstanding, he got himself elected and took his seat in the House. The pension, of course, he still continues to enjoy.

Where population is thick and the choice of companions large, as at an English University, quarrels are rare, for men can easily avoid uncongenial society. Where population is sparse, as up the country in a colony, jealousies and animosities are more likely to arise and to become inveterate. And thus the same kind of petty personal and party spirit which is to be found in the Parliament, often pervades to a still worse and more noxious extent the Municipal Councils which have the local management of the country districts. Roads, excellently engineered and solidly made in old days by convict labour, are allowed to get out of repair because there is a dispute in the Municipal Council whether or not a new road shall be made, which would be shorter for some and longer for others. Corrupt officials are retained because their patrons or relations are in a majority in the Council. In one instance which came under my notice, an upright and conscientious magistrate was so moved to indignation by the unpunished misconduct and peculations of the police superintendent of the district, that he could not refrain from denouncing him in a hustings speech. The offender retorted by publicly giving the magistrate the lie, there and then, and at the next petty sessions summoned the magistrate for slander, the magistrate at the same time taking out a cross summons against him for insulting his superior. There could not be a doubt of the man's guilt, though hitherto all attempts to punish him had failed, yet it was so notoriously certain to be made a party question, that when the magistrates assembled they confessed that they were not impartial enough to hear the case, and agreed to refer it to some magistrate of another district. Even then the two parties amongst the magistrates could not agree to whom to refer it, and at last were reduced to the expedient of selecting three magistrates' names by lot.

The Press of course suffers from the paucity of readers and from the absence of a sufficiency of topics to discuss. Every day one if not two leaders appear, often necessarily about nothing at all, while the rest of the sheet has to be filled up anyhow, with cases of vagrants fined at the police-court for being drunk, and so on. Hobart Town in general supports only one daily paper, though now and then another makes a start, which suffices for all the south of the island. There are no other gods in Olympus, and so this local Jupiter reigns with undisputed sway, his power being as independent of his merit as that of the Emperor of China. So entirely uncontrolled and uncriticised is it that even a Premier in forming an Administration may have to take account of it as of a formidable power in the state, which cannot be defied with impunity, and may even consider that it is entitled to be consulted on such matters, and be ready to resent anything having the appearance of neglect. In such a state of things there is of course always a possibility and a danger of the Jupiter for the time being falling into the hands of some ambitious, unscrupulous, and perhaps illiterate speculator, and being used by him as an instrument of personal advancement, as could easily be done in a hundred different ways, and so becoming a serious annoyance as a source of jobbery and petty tyranny. There is indeed a rival Olympus at Launceston in the north of the island. But there are generally two or three deities there to share the power between them, and moreover the northern and southern population have in many respects different interests, and do not, I believe, read each other's papers very much.

## VIII.

### TASMANIA (*continued*).

I MUST recall even the little I have said in a former letter in dispraise of the Tasmanian climate. In the valleys it may be too mild and enervating, but there are other parts where it is very different.

Go in the coach, for instance, for sixty miles along the high road to Launceston, which is still the main artery of the settlement, having been made in the old times, with enormous expenditure of labour, by huge gangs of convicts, clusters of whose ruined and deserted huts are still to be seen. It is by far the best road in all the Australian colonies, the only one (as far as I know) over which a common English stage-coach can travel, and travel too at the rate of ten miles an hour, including stoppages. Then mount your horse, leave highways and civilisation behind, and ride westwards along a pleasant grassy road to the foot of a long wooded range, or tier, as it is called. You ascend perhaps a thousand feet and find yourself, not on a ridge or a mountain, but on a high table-land, in a new and uninhabited country and in a new climate. It is the lake country. Five large lakes, from one to three thousand feet above the plains, are ready to pour down their waters and irrigate the whole island into a garden. The sun's rays are as powerful as on the plains, but the air is fresh and even keen, and at night for the greater part of the year it freezes sharply. Snow falls often as early as March, the first month of autumn. There is no fear of relaxing heat there. The grass is greener, too, and feels softer and more springy to ride over. A continuous fence is on each side of the track; for the country, though uninhabited except by sheep and their keepers, is most of it purchased and fenced now. But it is a dead-wood fence of unhewn trunks, with the smaller branches built up horizontally upon them, and therefore not an eyesore, like the ugly straight post-and-rail fences; and, moreover, capable of being easily cleared by a horse at any weak place. Eight miles of this, and a large and beautiful lake startles you by shining not a hundred yards off through the trees, and, almost at the same moment, another lake on the opposite side. Between them is a log hut, the first habitation passed for twenty miles, and out of it appears a fine, active-looking old man, whose privilege it is to stop passers-by for a ten minutes' chat. In Tasmania it is not safe to ask a stranger *why* he left home, but you may always ask *where* the old home was, and the old man is soon full of Oxford, and the boats, and boat races, and knows (alas!) which boat has been winning at Putney of late years. And so you may go on day after day. It may be there is nothing strikingly magnificent in this part of the country, but there is not a mile of the track that is not charming in its way. Only you must not lose it. For some distance the fences of the sheep-runs are parallel to and indicate it, and there is no fear of getting wrong, but afterwards you need some one who knows the country for a guide. For it is seldom that there are landmarks to go by. Once off the track, and there is nothing but the compass or the sun to steer by, and nothing bigger than a hut to aim at. One gum is like another gum, and one wattle like another wattle, and you may come back to the same spot without recognising it. And there is nothing to eat in the bush, unless by chance you come across a kangaroo, or an opossum, or a kangaroo-rat, and have the means to kill, and the inclination to eat, such food. In old times this part of the country was a favourite haunt of bushrangers, but want of food obliged them to make frequent incursions into the more settled districts, and in all the Australian colonies bushranging was, for this reason, easily extinguished, where it had not the connivance of some of the settlers. In New South Wales there must be a taste for preserving bushrangers, for they still flourish there.

Or if you prefer a more settled country with farms and townships at distant intervals, cross the broad deep Derwent by the steam-ferry at Hobart Town, or, taking the other road, by a ferry three or four miles higher up, of which a burly Yorkshireman has charge. The first road winds round a high hill, and the second mounts it by a gradual continuous ascent of three miles. The cleared land with its yellow harvest or green, growing crops, and neat dead-wood fences and bushes of luxuriant sweet-briar, and perhaps a garden and green English trees, make a foreground to a forest of gum-trees and wattles, which has been thinned but not cleared by fire, or by cutting a deep ring through the bark of the trees, for the sake of the scanty brown grass underneath, which their shade and growth make still more scanty. The bare white trunks and boughs of these slaughtered but still standing trees stand out grim and gaunt against the sky for many a year, till a pitying gale or a fire at their roots brings them to earth, making weird and ghostly dells such as Gustave Doré loves to draw, and too often needlessly caricatures. The road descends again upon a township. There is generally something dreary and repelling about the townships in all the Australian colonies. They are like little bits cut out of a modern English manufacturing town, and more than half killed in the process. Bare square-built brick houses, without a scrap of flower-garden or shrubbery, or any heed given to prettiness or neatness. Almost every tree cut down for perhaps a mile round; dust and glare; an inordinate number of public-houses, none of which care much to take you in unless you are a large consumer of strong drinks. They look like places intended only for business, and not for homes at all. And so you pass through a township, if possible, without stopping, and this time three miles on you turn aside across pleasant meadows to where, half hidden by St. Helena weeping willows and by a thick high hedge of brilliant yellow broom, stands a hospitable house. There is another house, the prettiest of wooden cottages, or rather bungalows, where you would be equally welcome; but you must leave it for another time, for if you stopped everywhere where you were tempted, you would not travel far in Tasmania. The road henceforth is in general only a track cleared, where it is necessary, amongst the trees; and you and your horse's feet rejoice in the absence of all pavement save nature's own. Day after day you ride on through the pleasant bush, meeting or passing or seeing some one perhaps once in two or three hours. Bright-coloured parrakeets fly about in flocks; the blue, red, and green Rosella parrot is the commonest bird of any in the bush. Now and then, though rarely, you may see a white cockatoo raise his yellow crest, or a kangaroo or wallaby jump across the track, or a mild-eyed opossum looks foolishly at you from a tree; or you stop to kill with a whip or stick a snake basking by the road-side, as you are bound to do if possible, for they are numerous and all poisonous. Of sounds there are few. Sometimes in the early morning the native magpie fills the air with the music of his delicious dreamy note, or later in the day the jackass utters his absurd laugh. The bush is monotonous perhaps, and the foliage and vegetation grey and brown and scanty, and the ground often bare instead of grassy, as in moister climates, but here there is constant change of hill and valley, constant pleasant surprises of new scenery, such as one meets with only in travelling for the first time in country undescribed by tourists and guide-books. If it spoils the interest of a novel to be told the plot beforehand, does it not ten times more spoil the enjoyment of new country to be forewarned of its surprises of scenery, which are the most delicious morsels of our pleasure in it? And along this east coast you seldom or never need a guide, for, wild and lonely as it often is, the track is always clear enough. You may, if you please, take a cart and luggage, for it is astonishing how carts and their horses learn to dispense with roads. A horse that is used to it thinks nothing of drawing a cart over a fallen trunk a couple of feet in diameter, going at it obliquely, one wheel at a time. But as tall hats, and black coats, and crinolines, and bonnets are about as necessary on a bush journey as an Armstrong gun or a pair of skates, you will probably dispense with any such useless incumbrance, and take only a change of clothes in a valise on the pommel of your saddle or behind it, or a mackintosh-covered bundle of eight or nine pounds weight strapped neatly to the off side of your side-saddle. You are free then, and can go or stay when and where the spirit moves you. And to anyone with the faintest idea how to use pencil or brush, the sharpness of outline, the clear blue of the distance, the brilliant sunshine and strong defined shadows, offer temptations to stop at every turn, and let your horse stand quietly grazing—'hung up,' as the phrase is, to a tree—while you sketch at leisure. You spend a day or two perhaps on Prosser's

Plains, a level tract lying charmingly amongst bush-covered hills; or turn aside to Cape Bougainville with its lovely views of the coast and of Maria Island; and you pass close along the calm shore of Oyster Bay, the sea a deep Prussian blue with broad dark lines of shadow, and beyond, closing in the bay, the bright purple island and peninsula of Schouten. A lovelier coast, and a less frequented, it would be hard to find. Hobart Town is seventy or eighty miles off, and there are no made roads to communicate with it. Formerly a small steamer plied thither, but somebody must needs start an opposition steamer, and so they ruined each other, and both ceased to ply, and now there is only a small schooner. Every fifteen or twenty miles, or oftener, you come to cleared land, often studded with stumps two or three feet high in the midst of the growing crops, and to the house of the proprietor generally built all on the ground-floor, and all the prettier and more comfortable in consequence, and almost always with a deep verandah, which gives it shadow and character. Properties are small and produce little, compared with the huge stations of the other colonies, and there is little prospect of acquiring great wealth. But, on the other hand, there is not the same Damocles-sword of anxiety lest a drought or a fall in the price of wool should bring inevitable bankruptcy and ruin. Here up the country one does not hear so much moaning and groaning as in the towns about the depressed state of the colony, which after all is for the most part only an undue hurry and impatience to get rich. Cannot people be satisfied with a fair profit on their own capital, without borrowing at eight or nine per cent., and expecting a large profit over and above on that? There may be too much wealth in a country for comfort and happiness, as well as too much poverty, if people would only believe it. Few things disturb honest industry and breed discontent more than the contemplation of too easily and too rapidly acquired fortunes. Those that were made in Victoria and elsewhere soon after the discovery of gold have left their demoralising and disheartening influence on all Australia. Without a large income, Arcadian luxury of climate, scenery, and quiet may be enjoyed in Tasmania. It is the perfection of retired country life. If there is in general not much wealth, there are almost always comfort and plenty. It does not matter that Hobart Town is some days' journey distant, and that a day's shopping is an occurrence that seldom happens once a year—sometimes not once in many years—for almost every want of the household is supplied from its own resources. And a traveller from the old country, utter stranger though he be, meets with a welcome so cordial, so hearty, so completely as a matter of course, that to one used only to the highways of European travel it bears a tinge almost of romance, and the memory of days thus spent in perfect enjoyment gathers a halo about it which no words of mine can describe.

Or ride out of Hobart Town, where, perhaps, towards the end of the summer scarcely any rain has fallen for two or three months, and follow the new road to the Huon, over the side of Mount Wellington. As you ascend, on a sudden it is cold and damp, and the road sloppy with wet. The vegetation, too, has changed. The gums are ten times the height of those down below, straight gigantic trunks, rising fifty to a hundred feet without a branch. People speak of trunks seventy feet in circumference twelve feet above the ground, but I have seen none so large as that. I am afraid to guess at their height: the mightiest European trees are dwarfs in comparison. Splitters are at work felling them and clearing away the underwood, and the blows of the axe sound and echo as if in a banqueting-hall of the gods. It is sacrilege to fell them; but the gaps made open out a view far away over the tops of the trees below to the mouths of the Derwent and the Huon, the jagged coast-line, the distant capes and breakwater-like islands, conspicuous amongst them, long, narrow Bruni, where Captain Cook landed nearly a century ago; and over all the south wind blows cool and fresh from the Southern Ocean, for there is nothing but sea and ice between you and the Pole. Further on the road diminishes to a narrow track, cut amongst the huge gums, and through an undergrowth of almost tropical vegetation so dense that within twelve miles of Hobart Town it remained till a few years ago almost unpenetrated. There is the sassafras, with straight, tapering stem and branches, and fragrant myrtle-like leaves; and fern trees, drooping their large graceful fronds from thick brown or red stems, from six to thirty feet high; and bright purple nightshade berries as big as cherries, and shrubs without end, and it seems almost without names, except such barbarous misapplications of English names as are in use to distinguish them, till the Heralds' Office of the Linnæan Society gives them title, rank, and lineage—all growing in a dense mass, and baffling even the all-penetrating sun. Then the track descends a little, and it all vanishes, and the ground is dry as before, and two hours' more riding brings you out suddenly upon the bank of a fine river, the Huon, as wide here and deeper than the Thames at Richmond. A short distance off along the bank are a roughly made landing-stage and a ferry boat, and you must *cooé* in the best falsetto you can (if there is a lady of the party she will probably do it better) till the ferryman hears you and comes, and with some trouble persuades the horses into the boat, and punts you across, and gives you directions how to thread your way through the scrub till you emerge upon a corduroy road and upon the township of Franklin. It is the chief township of the district, with some six hundred inhabitants, exceptional in being the perfection of a country village, stretching along the base of a hill two or three hundred feet high, and fringing the river bank and tiny wharf with its neat wooden houses. The grass is green, and not burnt up and brown, as it is in most places long before summer is over, for here there is moisture enough all the year round. The people here grow apples, and send them off by shiploads straight from the wharf to the all-devouring Melbourne market; and they make shingles for roofing, and shape timber, and saw up the famous Huon pine, which they often have not even the trouble of felling, for the winter floods wash it down from almost unpenetrated bush. Though it is not thirty miles from Hobart Town and civilization, yet westward for seventy or eighty miles to the sea is no human habitation, nothing but bush so thick, so devoid of anything to support life, that of the convicts who from time to time in years past escaped into it from Macquarie Harbour, on the west coast, scarcely any got through alive. Much of it needs only clearing to make fine agricultural land. There are millions of acres to be bought by the first comer at a pound an acre. Yet, out of sixteen and a half million acres which Tasmania contains, only three and a half are alienated, and on this small portion, including the towns, the population is less than one person for thirty-five acres!

Can any country be more perfectly delightful? Once mounted (and, rich or poor, there are few who cannot possess or borrow a horse of some sort in Tasmania) one is free with a freedom known only in dreams to dwellers in the old country of hedges and Enclosure Acts, where to quit the dreary flinty roads is to trespass and to break the law. One's first reflection is on the astonishing folly of humanity in neglecting to inhabit it. Surely there must be many wearied with the crowd and strife and ugliness of

English cities, who, brought to a virgin forest such as this, would be ready to sing their *Nunc dimittis* in thankfulness that it had been permitted them to exist in such beauty, to have their dreams helped to the imagination of the glory of the new heavens and the new earth. Probably, however, not one person in twenty, take England through, would have his or her enjoyment of life materially increased by living in a free unspoiled country, with abundance of space and air, or indeed in natural beauty of any kind; and doubtless a large majority at heart prefer the shops of Oxford Street, for a continuance, to the most beautiful scenery imaginable. And it may be there is something of a true instinct in them, such as was in Sir Robert Peel when (as the story goes) he used to stand at the top of Trafalgar Square, and looking down over the dreary, ugly, blackened buildings, and the busy colourless crowd, say it was the most beautiful sight he ever saw. For after all men are better than trees. Besides, rich people are too comfortable to change their homes and their hemisphere, and poor people must go where they can find bread as well as beauty. So till the country is found to provide a cure for impecuniosity as well as for less tangible and less generally recognised requirements, it must remain, I suppose, nearly as it is.

The common, and no doubt correct, reason given for its failure in this last respect, is that it is essentially an agricultural and not a pastoral country, owing to the quantity of timber, and that wheat is too cheap to repay even a moderate profit on cultivation. Wheat is unnaturally cheap now, because the popular cry in Victoria lately has been for protection, and the Victorian Government, to conciliate it, and to nurse their 'cockatoo' settlers, has put a duty on corn and other produce which, to a great extent, drives the Tasmanians from their natural and legitimate market. Certainly, at the present low prices, a farmer employing labourers finds it difficult to make a living. In some places there is land thrown out of cultivation, looking dismal enough. Nevertheless, for common agricultural labourers there is plenty of demand; a labourer can earn at least three times as much as he can in the southern counties of England. In wages he gets at least ten shillings a week, out of which he has hardly anything but his clothes to buy; for in addition he has rations, consisting of twelve pounds of mutton, twelve pounds of flour, two pounds of sugar, and a quarter of a pound of tea; and a log hut, and a garden if he likes, rent free. Fresh comers from England sometimes do not know how to consume so large an allowance of meat, and ask to have part of it changed for something else. But before long they fall into the universal Tasmanian custom of eating meat three times a day, and learn to be glad of it all. At shearing time a large number of hands are wanted at once, and wages are much higher. It is a common thing for a man after shearing is over to give the cheque he has earned, perhaps for twenty pounds or more, to the keeper of the nearest grog-shop, and bid him supply him with liquor there and then till it is all spent. If a man will only keep from drink he can save money enough in a few years to buy land and support himself till his first crop is reaped. He has no labour to pay for, and like the peasant proprietors of Adelaide, who this year have been sending their wheat to England, may succeed where an employer of labour fails. There is land along the north coast rich as any in the world, but heavily timbered. The settler gets rid of the smaller trees and underwood simply by setting it on fire, and sows his seed in the ashes, and gets a fine crop without even ploughing, leaving the larger timber to be felled as he has leisure for it. There are harbours all along this coast, and a railway is about to be made, and before many years are over it will take a heavy tariff to keep the produce of this fertile district out of Melbourne market.

And after all, at the worst, is it to come to this— that a shrewd, strong, hard-working man, with plenty of land of his own, cannot live unless markets and prices are favourable? Need an Englishman starve now, under circumstances in which a Saxon or a Dane of a thousand years ago would, after his fashion, have luxuriated in plenty? If so, it is the custom of excessive subdivision of labour, the growing incompleteness in themselves of men and of households, which has spoilt us for settling in a new country. Such subdivision of course increases production in a highly civilised country, but it may easily become a source of mental and physical degradation to the producer.

Sheffield knives may be the best and cheapest in the world, but we have all heard of the Sheffield emigrant girl, who, landing in a new colony, and seeking employment, confessed she had never been taught to do anything whatever, indoors or outdoors, but *pack files.* If wheat or other produce will not fetch a profit, cannot a man grow less of it, and instead keep sheep and poultry to supply himself with meat, and on such a soil as this grow perhaps grapes for his own wine, such as it is, and even possibly flax for his own linen? And if his wife be of the right sort for a settler's wife, and not of the file-packing sort, there will be few things for which he need go to a shop. Such a state of things, if possible, and not Utopian, has at least this advantage, that it saves the wife and young children from the great bane of peasant proprietorship, that of becoming like mere unthinking, routine-following beasts of burden on the soil, as we see them too often in Belgium and France, with no other thought or employment but how to put the utmost possible pound of manure on the soil, and how to extract from it the utmost bushel in return, to the neglect of all things else on earth. At any rate, it is hardly to be believed that English agricultural labourers will not, sooner or later, have spirit to attempt to solve the problem for themselves one way or another, rather than rest contented with their present condition. The present generation may hope to live to see them asking twice or three times their present wages, and, if unable to obtain them, departing for a new, and, for them, a freer country.

Unfortunately, some working men at home have singularly unpractical ideas about freedom. At least so it appears to us out here at the antipodes, where home questions assume such different relative proportions, and the monthly mail, with its tale of political strife, is so often a weariness rather than a pleasure to read. Franchise questions are trifles compared to land questions out here, and we cannot see the point (even after allowing for rhetorical flourish) of people choosing to call themselves serfs because they have not got votes. It is difficult to understand what conceivable meaning those men could have attached to the word 'freedom,' who considered that they were asserting or claiming it by parading the streets at the summons of a Beales. To us, such an exhibition of franchise-worship—if that be what it means—under such a high priest, appears like lingering round a golden calf, when a promised land lies waiting to be claimed.

## IX.

### SYDNEY AND ITS NEIGHBOURHOOD.

The chief towns of the five principal Australian Colonies are separated by nearly equal intervals. The distances from Adelaide to Melbourne, from Melbourne to Hobart Town, from Melbourne to Sydney, and from Sydney to Brisbane are not very different. That from Melbourne to Sydney is a little the longest of them. It is rather more than a two days' and two nights' voyage. To go by land is a tedious and laborious journey, except for those who know the country and its inhabitants very well. Only a small portion can be done by railway, and most of the way is through flat, monotonous country, more or less afflicted with floods, bushrangers, bad roads, and worse inns. Indeed, whenever there is steam communication by water between two Australian towns, it is seldom that there is any other practicable way of going.

The Melbourne steamer keeps close in shore all the way. The coast generally has a barren look, and, except at Cape Schank and near a mountain called the Pigeon House, has few striking features. It is so little settled or cultivated that its appearance from the sea cannot be much changed since Captain Cook explored it. It is seldom that there is a sail in sight. At the very entrance of Port Jackson hardly a living creature, few buildings except the lighthouses, and no mast of a ship at anchor are visible. It is not till the narrow opening between the high precipitous cliffs is entered and the South Head rounded, that a scene of beauty bursts upon you as suddenly as a vision in a fairy story. In an instant the long rollers and angry white surf (for there are rollers and surf on the shores of the Pacific on the calmest day) are left behind, and the vessel is gliding smoothly over a glassy lake, doubly and trebly land-locked, so that the open sea is hidden from every part of it. To the north and east numberless inlets and coves branch off, subdivide, and wind like rivers between rocky scrub-covered shores, which are fragrant with wattle, and brilliant with wild flowers, all new and strange to a European eye. To the left, on the southern side, are large deep bays, on the shores of which the rich men of Sydney have built villas and planted gardens, with which no villa or garden at Torquay or at Spezzia can compare. Farther on, perhaps four miles from the Heads, you pass three or four men-of-war, lying motionless at anchor little more than a couple of stone-throws from the shore, having for their background the graceful bamboos, and trim Norfolk Island and Moreton Bay pines, and palms, and other semi-tropical vegetation of the Botanic Gardens. Steamers of all sizes, from the great P. and O. and Panama ocean steamship, to the busy, puffing, gaily-painted little harbour paddle-boat, plough up the clear water. Pleasure boats, from the yacht to the sculler's funny, flit noiselessly about. Or a panting steam-tug drags a merchant ship amongst the hulls and masts and funnels which fringe the innermost part of the harbour. Above the masts, with miles of winding wharfage at its base, stands Sydney. At sunrise or sunset on a calm day there is something almost Oriental in the brilliancy of colour, something dreamy and unsubstantial in the water, the shores, the black hulls and spars, seen through the sun-lit haze, like pictures one sees of the Golden Horn—such as Turner would have delighted to paint. Port Jackson, both for use and beauty, is almost unsurpassed in the world. It is nowhere much more than a mile in width; its most distant extremities are not twenty miles apart in a straight line; yet its perimeter, measured along the water's edge and up its numberless little inlets, must be hundreds of miles in length.

But once land and enter the town itself, and all pleasing prospects and illusions vanish at once. Never was a city less worthy of its situation. The principal street is nearly two miles long. For the greater part of the way this street is more or less in a hollow, and from hardly any part of it is the harbour visible. The rest of the city straggles right and left of it, covering with its suburbs a very large extent of ground. Only one good street, Macquarie Street, is finely situated. There are two really fine buildings, superior to anything of the kind in Melbourne, the new Cathedral, and the Hall of the University. A few public buildings and some of the banks are solidly, if not gracefully, built. But in general the houses are small, ugly, ill drained, ill built, and in bad repair, and the greater part of the town a poor specimen of the mean style of house architecture prevailing in England forty or fifty years ago. It is but seldom that any attempt has been made to make the plans of houses such as to suit the requirements of the climate, as has been done so successfully at Melbourne. Deep verandahs, which add so much to the appearance of a building by producing contrasts of light and shade, and which are so essential to comfort in a hot, glaring climate, are the exception rather than the rule. People who can afford to be comfortable and luxurious live out of town now, and so what is perhaps the best part of Sydney has been preserved almost unaltered from the Governor-Macquarie era of half a century ago.

The climate is such as to make shade and protection from sun, wind, and dust almost a necessity. In winter, in July and August for instance, it is very pleasant. Even then it is often as hot in the sun as on an average fine day in England in summer; and a fire is out of the question, except in the evening or on a wet day. Snow has not fallen in Sydney, it is said, for twenty years. A sensation was produced the other day by a large snow-ball which a guard on the railway brought in his van from somewhere up the country where there had been a snow-storm. Towards the end of September it begins to be unpleasantly hot. The streets are for the most part left unwatered. Often a violent hot wind blows, filling the air with fine red dust, which penetrates through closed doors and windows, covering everything, and severely trying all mucous membranes, eyes, and tempers. This wind is known as a *Brickfielder*. It blows from the west, and generally lasts from one to two days. Then comes a southerly wind, often accompanied by rain and thunder, which strikes it at right angles, and prevails over it. The temperature at once falls. The sea breeze is disliked by many almost as much as the other, for though cool it is enervating. The temperature in summer at Sydney is not nearly so high as in the interior. Yet the Squatter from up the country when he comes there complains of the heat. Labourers declare that they cannot do a good day's work there. With all classes hours of work are short and holidays frequent. Old people and persons with delicate and peculiar constitutions may have their lives prolonged; but strong men get ill who never were ill before, and complexions and faces look white, sallow, and shrunken almost like those of Anglo-Indians.

Sydney is specially deserving of attention as being politically a fair average type of an Australian city. It is more like what most other Australian towns are likely to become than any other place. For the colony is nearly eighty years old. It has a history by no means uneventful or uninteresting. Among its early heroes it can point to many men of conspicuous ability, energy, and integrity. Most of the population are natives of the colony, real colonials, and not emigrants from the old country. They are less restless, less excitable, perhaps less energetic, than their neighbours at Melbourne. Some of them have hardly ever been ten miles from their native city.

Though no longer the capital or even the first city of Australia, Sydney is an important and increasing town. The more rapid growth of Melbourne has thrown it into the shade, and no doubt Melbourne will maintain its position, and, owing to its central situation, continue to be the commercial emporium of the other colonies. But it may be doubted whether Victoria will maintain its lead over New South Wales. The good land of Victoria extends to the very shores of Port Phillip, the country is small comparatively, and has been easily opened up. In New South Wales three trunk lines are in progress and are open for some distance, but hundreds of miles of railway must be made before many fertile districts can be even known, except by report, and before even the inhabitants—much more, possible emigrants at home—begin to realise the enormous resources of the country. Gold is found in all directions, though as yet in few places, compared with Victoria, in quantities which repay the digger. Iron is plentiful. There is an unlimited supply of coal close to the mouth of the Hunter. Kerosene is being procured in abundance. The English cereals flourish as well as maize and arrowroot. Almost any quantity of wine might be grown, and some of it is about as good as average light French claret. Light wine is a great addition to comfort in this climate; and as it becomes more plentiful, and cheaper, it will help more than anything to drive out the old colonial vice of excessive spirit-drinking, already on the decline. There are several varieties of climate, for climate depends more upon height above the sea-level than upon latitude. From the mountainous district of Kiandra the telegraph day after day even to the end of September reports 'snow falling,' while at Sydney we are broiling. In New England, close to the borders of Queensland, there is almost an English climate, and strawberries and other English fruits and vegetables grow in perfection; while a short distance off, on the Clarence, and on the vast plains to the westward, the heat, though dry and comparatively healthy, is intense, and men will put away their coats and waistcoats in a box, only to be taken out if they want to go to Sydney or to look specially respectable. To the number of sheep and cattle which may be kept there is practically no limit. Only there is a distance beyond which the expense of carting wool or driving cattle to a market eats up all the profit. For wool, railways will at once extend this distance. As for cattle, there is a new invention for freezing meat by means of ammonia, and thus preserving it entirely unchanged for any number of weeks or months. If this is successful, as there is every reason to hope, frozen meat may be brought down to the nearest port and kept frozen for a voyage of any length, and thus the English market may be supplied with fresh meat from the heart of Australia.

Food, both animal and vegetable, is perhaps as cheap in Australia as in any part of the world. Even in Sydney, where it is comparatively dear, the best beef and mutton cost only about fourpence a pound, a price which is said to pay a very large profit to the butcher. Inferior meat is as low as a penny or twopence a pound. Wheat this year has been as low as half-a-crown a bushel in some country places. In the bush, where shepherds and others get their rations of half a sheep each a week, the waste is often very great. Much is thrown away, or given to the dogs, or spoilt by bad cooking. This abundance makes it at first sight seem extraordinary that the early settlers at Sydney should have been for so many years dependent on supplies of salt provisions brought from England or the Cape, and that when these supplies ran short they should several times have been on the verge of starvation. But a ride outside the town explains it. The soil for many miles round is sandy and barren. To this day unenclosed and uncultivated land extends up to the very streets of the town. Even market gardeners have not found it worth while to establish themselves, except in a few gullies where the soil is a little better. It is a good thing *now* that this is so; for near a large city, which can easily be supplied from a distance, an unlimited expanse of natural park is better than ploughed fields. Populous and straggling as the town is, a short ride, or half an hour's row across the harbour, takes you into country as wild as a Scotch moor. On the north shore you may almost lose yourself in the bush within two or three miles of the town. To the south you may ride in an hour and a half over glorious open country, amongst scarlet bottle-brush, epacris, and a profusion of beautiful wild flowers, to the clear water and white, sandy, uninhabited shores of Botany Bay, which even in mid-winter quite deserves its name.

Amongst the few cultivated districts near Sydney is Parramatta. It is there that the trim gardens of dark green orange trees are, with their profusion of golden fruit hanging patiently among the leaves for three or four months. But to see agriculture on a large scale you must go by railway nearly thirty miles to the valley of the Hawkesbury. A richer alluvial soil than there is in this valley could not well be, nor one requiring less labour in its cultivation. But, owing to droughts and floods, so precarious are the crops that the cultivators are said to be content if they can secure one out of three which they sow. In the early days a bad flood on the Hawkesbury caused a scarcity throughout the colony. In June last an unusually bad one occurred. The river actually rose nearly sixty feet in perpendicular height, flowing more than forty feet above the roadway of the bridge near Richmond. You may see the rubbish brought down by it on the tops of the trees. And though the stream runs between high banks, the wide, flat plain above was twelve feet deep in rushing water, which a furious gale of wind made still more destructive. A few small patches are already green again with a luxuriant crop. The rest of the plain is a dismal brown expanse of dried mud. The strong post-and-rail fences are tumbling down or half buried. Here and there a few slabs or a door-post sticking up out of the ground mark the place from which a log hut or a cottage has been swept away.

Another fertile district, the Illawarra, may be reached by going in a coasting steamer for fifty miles south from Sydney. A longer but pleasanter way is to take the Southern Railway for thirty-five miles, and ride the remaining thirty. The ride is through poor, sandy, scrubby country, abounding, as sandy soils so often do, with brilliant wild flowers. The native or gigantic lily grows here in perfection, a single red flower on a straight stem, often fifteen or twenty feet high; and the waratah, or native tulip, in diameter as big as a sunflower, but conical, and crimson like a peony. Suddenly you reach the edge of a steep descent, so steep as to be almost a cliff, and look down amongst large timber trees interlaced with dark-leaved creepers of almost tropical growth, which hang like fringed ropes from the trunks and branches. Lower down are palms, wild figs, and cabbage palms; and beyond is a broad strip of rich green meadow land, lying far below between the cliff and the sea, and stretching many miles away to the south. Half an hour's steep descent takes you down to it. There is a home-like look about the green grass, the appearance of prosperity, and the substantial look of the farm houses. Farmers' wives jog along to Wollongong market with their baskets or their babies before them on the pommels of their saddles. Almost everybody, except a few of the larger landowners, is Irish. Here, if anywhere, the Irish have fallen upon pleasant places and found congenial occupation. There is very little agriculture. The land is all in pasture, and nothing is kept but cows. The population is wholly given up to making butter. Even cheese they do not condescend to make; but Wollongong butter is the butter of Sydney, and finds its way to far-off places along the coast. The meadows are as green in summer as in winter, or even greener. For then the sea breeze often brings heavy showers and storms, and droughts are seldom known there. I saw an English oak tree in full leaf in the middle of August—the February of the southern hemisphere. So valuable is the land, that as much as 20*l.* an acre has been given for uncleared land, and 2*l.* a year rent—prices almost unheard of in Australia.

But the pleasantest of all the short journeys to be made from Sydney is to the Blue Mountains. The range is not high, in few places, I believe, more than three thousand feet above the sea; but it is intersected by very deep precipitous ravines, and densely wooded; and the chain, or rather mass, of mountainous country is very wide. It was many years before the early colonists succeeded in penetrating it and getting at the good country beyond. Even now there is only one road and one cattle track across it. After the first ascent at the Kurrajong the track descends a little, and then runs nearly level for twelve miles till Mount

Tomer is reached, on the highest ridge, beyond which the water-shed is to the south-west. Here, as at the Illawarra, occurs one of those sudden changes which are so delightful in the midst of the monotony of the bush. The ragged, close-growing, insignificant, 'never-green' gum-trees, which, mixed with a few wattles (*mimosa*) and she-oaks, are the principal constituents of *bush*, give place to enormous trees of the same as well as of other species. The delicate light green of the feathery tree-ferns relieves the eye. The air is full of aromatic scent from many kinds of shrubs, all growing luxuriantly. Wherever there is an opening you can see as far as the coast, and for nearly a hundred miles to the north and to the south, over the bush you have come through. And seen at a distance, the poorest bush has a peculiar and beautiful colour, quite different from anything we see in Europe, a reddish ground, shaded with the very deepest blue, often without a trace of green.

Sheep, it is said, do not thrive east (that is, on the Sydney side) of the Blue Mountains, till as far northwards as the rich valley of the Hunter. As for cattle, I was told that the quickest and easiest way to get to a cattle station from Sydney was to take a voyage of two days and two nights in a steamer to Brisbane, in Queensland, and thence go a day's journey by railway to the Darling Downs. For New South Wales is a vast country, and distances from place to place very great. Railways as yet do not extend far. Roads are very bad, seldom metalled, often only tracks. In the valley of the Hunter, on the great northern road, a road as much frequented and as important as any in the colony, I have seen twenty oxen yoked to one dray to drag it through the mud up a hill which was neither very steep nor very long. The coaches in New South Wales, as in Victoria, are all of the American kind, low and broad, resting on very long leather straps stretched taut longitudinally, which are the substitutes for springs. An ordinary English coach would very soon have its springs broken and be upset. They generally have (as they need to have) very good drivers, many of whom are Yankees or Canadians. The bodily exertion and endurance required for a long coach journey are not small. The ruts and holes made by the narrow wheels of the drays are often so deep as to make it advisable to leave the road for a mile or two, and drive straight through the bush amongst the trees. Often the best way of getting through a bad place is to go at it at a gallop. Everybody holds tight to save his hat and his bones, and when the difficulty is passed the driver looks round at his passengers and asks enquiringly, 'All aboard?' The horses, rough in appearance, possess wonderful strength and endurance. In spite of all difficulties, four horses will generally take a heavy crowded coach six or seven miles an hour, which is quite as fast as it is pleasant to travel on leather springs and on such roads. They are often used at first with little or no breaking-in. One day the driver of a mail coach meeting ours stopped us to ask if we had seen anything of his two leaders. They had broken loose from the rest of the team, he said, during the journey the night before, and got clear away, splinter-bars and all, and he had not seen or heard of them since.

## X.

### AN INSTITUTION OF NEW SOUTH WALES.

In New South Wales a considerable proportion of the population is of convict descent. It is impossible to say *what* proportion, for the line of separation is no longer strictly preserved, as it once was, between free settlers and emancipists; and questions are not often asked nowadays about origin and parentage. The tendency of the convicts when they got their liberty was to go to the country districts, rather than to the towns. Many became shepherds or hutkeepers on remote stations. Their children born in the bush have grown up with less instruction, religious or secular, often in even worse companionship, and with a still worse political education, than their fathers. For who was to look after them? Squatters, even if they had the will to do so, were few and far between, and Squatters' wives fewer still. The Voluntary System does not supply clergymen where there is no demand, although common sense and common experience show that where there is the least demand there is the sorest need. Those who remain of the convicts sent from England are old men now, except a few who have come across from Tasmania, for it is more than a quarter of a century since the last shipload of them entered Port Jackson. But they have left a legacy behind them which is emphatically the 'peculiar institution' of New South Wales, as distinguished from the other Australian colonies—*Bushranging*.

In the old times bushrangers were simply escaped prisoners, often desperate ruffians, who took life, when it suited them, without scruple. Even then they were not regarded as we regard thieves and murderers in England. Familiarity with criminals had taught the more humane among the settlers to consider them as men of like passions with themselves, and not as only pariahs and enemies of the human race. I have heard an eye-witness describe the 'sticking-up' of a house in the country many years ago. One of the bushrangers, without any warning, deliberately shot a manservant in the kitchen through the window. The lady of the house, hearing the report, ran into the kitchen and found the man badly shot in the arm. The bushranger who had shot him, instead of setting to work to plunder with his companions, at once came to her assistance, obeyed her directions, fetched water, and the two were amicably engaged for a long time binding up the wounded limb and assisting the sufferer. The gang were nearly all taken and hanged afterwards, but I think the people of this house felt more pity than satisfaction at their fate.

Many of the lower class have hardly disguised their sympathy with these successful outlaws. There is a tinge of romance about their lives. A bushranger is a greater and a freer man than a Hounslow highwayman of a century ago. He rides an excellent horse, and leads another by his side. He is armed with a 'six-shooter,' and perhaps with a rifle as well. He has miles and miles of country to roam over, and many a hut where fear or sympathy will at any time provide him with food or a night's lodging. Boys at school play at bushrangers, and no boy, if he can help it, will act the inglorious part of policeman. Even the name of the profession has been dignified by being turned into Latin. There is an inscription in the principal church of Sydney to some one *a latrone vagante occiso.*

And so it has come to pass that bushranging, which languished, or was kept under by the help of an efficient police, for many years, has broken out again with as great vigour as ever. The country is distributed between different gangs. I asked the driver of the Wollongong Mail if he had ever been 'stuck up.' His reply was, 'Not for nearly a year,' or something to that effect. On the main north road, along which you seldom travel a mile without meeting somebody, the mail coach was stopped at one o'clock in the day by a single armed man, who calls himself Thunderbolt, and carries on his depredations in this district. He compelled the driver to drive off the road into the bush, and there deliberately took down the mail bags and carried them off on a led horse. A few days later he unexpectedly came upon a policeman, who at once fired at him. He had just time to cover himself behind a horse he was leading; the bullet struck the led horse, and he escaped on the one he was riding. Less than three weeks after the first robbery he again stopped the same mail coach and the same driver, almost at the same place; this time at night. The account in the Sydney paper was as follows:—

> The down mail from Muswellbrook to Singleton, with two days' mails, was stuck up by Thunderbolt this morning at 3 o'clock, between Grasstree Hill and the Chain of Ponds. With the exception of one bag, all the letters were taken by him. The police are in pursuit.
> The weather is very warm.*

There is an unconscious irony in the way the hot weather and the robbery of Her Majesty's mail stand side by side, as if they were equally every-day matters. Generally a bushranging story only gets into small type in a corner of the paper, and very seldom indeed inspires a leading article. You may sometimes see two or three such accounts in a single daily paper. The most formidable gang is in the Lower Murrumbidgee, and is known as 'Blue Cap's' gang. I should like to quote unabridged a column of the newspaper in which some of their doings are described, but it is too long. It describes † how in the course of about a fortnight they ' stuck up' two mails, two public-houses (shooting at the owner of one, but fortunately not hitting him), a steamer on the river, and four stations, taking all

---

\* *Sydney Morning Herald*, October 9, 1867.

† *Sydney Morning Herald*, August 28, 1867, copied from the *Wagga Wagga Express* of August 24. 'Blue Cap' has since been taken, and his gang broken up. Thunderbolt (November 1868) still continues his career.

money, arms, horses, and valuables they found. Only one man, a mail-man, made serious resistance. He was mounted, and carried a large duelling pistol in each sleeve, and a revolver in his belt. Finding he was outnumbered, he fled, closely pursued by two of the gang, who soon overhauled him. Pistol shots were exchanged in quick succession, the horses going all the time at full speed. In the end, the mail-man, after wounding 'Blue Cap' in the hand, had come to his last barrel, when his horse fell with him, and he was at the mercy of his assailants. 'Blue Cap' was for giving him ten minutes to prepare for death and then shooting him; but his life was spared at the entreaty of a woman and of one of the gang who was friendly to him. A very pretty 'sensation' story this, one would have thought, and rather a catch for an editor. But no; it is a stale subject. And so the newspaper, for want of something better, had a leader on the expenses of Greenwich Hospital.

This wholesale plundering of houses and stations does not often happen. Operations are nowadays generally confined to the road. And usually no violence is offered except in resisting capture. For unless a bushranger has already forfeited his life by committing murder he will abstain from taking life if he can, being pretty sure that for any number of highway robberies unaccompanied with violence he will only be punished, at the worst, with penal servitude for life, and that if he behaves well in prison he may very likely be at large again in ten years. The owner of a house which is attacked must resist if he has much to lose which he cannot spare. But in travelling, people generally prefer to take little that is valuable with them, and to leave their pistols at home. For the bush which borders all the roads, more or less, gives the bushranger an almost irresistible advantage. He can choose his own position, and without being seen cover a driver or a passenger with his rifle or his revolver, and bid him throw up his arms or be shot, before the latter has time to get at his pistol. The traveller cannot be prepared on the instant. To undergo the jolts and plunges of an Australian coach on Australian roads with a cocked pistol in one's hand would be to run a greater risk than any to be apprehended from bushrangers. They practise, too, a certain contemptuous Turpin-like courtesy towards passengers, especially poor ones and women; and often take nothing but the mails. And so the actual loss and danger from this state of things is not so great as might be supposed. But the insubordinate and lawless spirit of the population, of which it is the evidence, is a more serious matter. And it must prevail very widely. A bushranger's person and features are generally perfectly well known in the district where he carries on his depredations. A large reward is offered for his capture. He could not get food to support him or clothes to wear without the connivance of a great number of persons. *With* their connivance he often pursues a successful career for years; and it is often only by a lucky accident if the police succeed in making a capture.

## XI.

#### POLITICAL DIFFICULTIES OF NEW SOUTH WALES.

IF the British public is as ignorant of other things as it is about Australia, it must be quite as ignorant a public as Mr. Matthew Arnold would have us believe. It appears to be under an impression that Australians habitually carry revolvers. It has always persisted in believing that Botany Bay was the place to which convicts were sent out, and has a misty idea that that much libelled bay is the port of Sydney. A person at Hobart Town is requested by an English friend to invite to dinner occasionally a man who lives at Sydney. Even Lord Grey invariably spells Port Phillip with one L. And so on. But the most remarkable blunder I have seen was made by the *Saturday Review*. It had an article criticising the appointment of Lord Belmore to the office of 'Governor-General of the Australian Colonies,' in blissful ignorance that no such office exists, or has existed for some years past. The office referred to was that of Governor of New South Wales. But it was not only a mistake in a name. The writer laid so much stress on the paramount importance of the appointment and the power it conferred, that it is evident that he was under the impression that a Governor residing at Sydney possesses authority over the other Australian colonies. I need hardly say that this is no more true than it is true that the Queen possesses authority over the United States of America.

On the all-important land question, legislation has not been much better in New South Wales than in Victoria. Here, as there, the 'Free Selectors' by force of numbers can carry elections and bend everything in their favour. The vicious system of balloting for blocks of land has not been introduced; for the extent of the country and thinness of the population have made the number of applicants for land in any one district comparatively few. On the other hand, not merely certain surveyed areas, as in Victoria, but the whole country, with the exception of small reserves, is open to free selection at a fixed price at any time. More than that, if a Squatter wishes to purchase a piece of his own run, even if no one else has expressed any desire to purchase it, he must give the requisite public notice to the Government officer, and then any other person who does not possess land may step in and buy the piece at the regulation price in preference to him. Thus, a Selector, made aware by the Squatter's notice of the portion of his run which he values most, may (and sometimes does) purchase it as a speculation, in the hope of annoying him into buying him off in a few years at an increased price. Every Squatter who leases a run from the Crown is liable to invasion by

Free Selectors. An abatement of rent is indeed made in case of land being taken from him, but the compensation is quite inadequate to the loss and injury sustained. For the Selector has grazing rights over a certain area in addition to the fee-simple of his block of land, and as he is under no obligation to fence, there is nothing to prevent his stock from feeding all over the Squatter's run. I was told that in some districts it has been found impossible to carry on cattle stations, and they have been abandoned or turned into sheep stations, owing to the Selectors. It was notorious that the latter, having in general little skill in agriculture, and being far from any market, could exist only by eating or selling the Squatters' cattle. Indeed this was pretty well proved by their often disappearing altogether from the neighbourhood when the keeping of cattle was given up. With sheep it is not quite so bad. They are under the shepherd's eye, and are sooner missed. And according to the bush code of morality, in some districts cattle are almost *feræ naturæ*, and taking them is not stealing in the same degree as taking a pocket handkerchief or even a sheep is.

A large proportion of the small settlers and Free Selectors in New South Wales are Irish. The English and Scotch in the Australian colonies amalgamate easily. They have no national or religious antipathies to overcome, and frequently even attend each other's churches. The Irish remain apart. They generally are glad to get a government situation of any kind, and are said to make very good officials, and they contribute the great majority of domestic servants. One does not hear of many of them being in trade. The greater number seem to go up the country, as they are generally desirous of becoming possessors of land, often in larger quantities than they can turn to profitable account. This desire once accomplished, which is a very easy matter in New South Wales, their ambition seems to be too readily satisfied. There seems no reason why a small settler should not earn money enough to live in comfort and even luxury by occasionally combining labour for wages with the cultivation of his own land. But, for what reason I know not, it is seldom that anything like comfort is to be seen amongst this class up the country. A man will just run up a rude slab hut for himself and his family, often with room enough between the slabs to put a hand through. The roof is easily made with sheets of bark tied on. Sometimes there is not even a window, and only one hole in the roof for the light to come in and the smoke to go out at. The floor is the bare ground, good enough in dry weather, in wet weather very likely killing off a child or two with consumption or rheumatic fever. The bread they eat is sometimes so bad and so sour that it is impossible for anyone unused to it to digest it, though any good bushman can make a damper in the ashes as sweet and wholesome as possible. Their mutton is often half wasted, and the rest cooked to the consistency of leather. The bones are thrown away, for who ever heard of soup or broth in the bush? It is too much trouble to grow vegetables. I went to one 'accommodation-house' (an inferior kind of inn), where there was a cow and plenty of milk, but it was too much trouble to drive her in to be milked, or even to tie up her calf so that she might not stray; and so all the children, two or three of whom were down with the measles, drank their bad tea, which is the staple beverage at all meals, and was especially needed here to disguise the abominable dirtiness of the water, without a drop of milk to it. Why are not children taught a little about kitchen economy and cooking at school? In the bush reading and writing are elegant and refined accomplishments, useful in their way, but mere ornamental accessories to a complete education compared with the knowledge how to make a loaf of bread and cook a bit of mutton.

De Tocqueville remarked on the depression and melancholy expressed on the countenance of the American backwoodsman and the harassed, prematurely aged look of the wife. Something of this is to be seen in the settler in the bush. You seldom see a smile or hear a laugh. It is not that there is any need to work harder than is good for health. Still less is there anything approaching to want. But the great loneliness is very trying to most minds. I have been told by a shepherd's wife that she did not see anyone but her husband much oftener than once in three months, and he was generally away all day, and often all night. Possibly she may have exaggerated a little. But this was within four miles of a township and a main road. What must it be in remote districts, where stations are sometimes twenty miles and more apart? Shepherding is the most lonely occupation of any, and it is said that a large proportion of the inmates of colonial lunatic asylums have been shepherds. If you ask anyone not born in the colony if he or she would like to go home again, not one in twenty but will wistfully and unhesitatingly answer 'Yes;' though not one in twenty but is richer and has greater means of living in comfort now than before leaving home. Not but what it would be a mistake to make too much of this preference for the old home. Happy memories live while sad ones perish, and those whom you ask are old now, probably, and were young when they were at home, and what they really mean (though they don't exactly know it) is that they liked being young better than they like being old.

The Irish here, as everywhere, multiply much faster than the rest of the population. It is said that at one time great efforts were made to swamp the rest of the population with Irish emigrants, and make New South Wales essentially a Roman Catholic colony. There is no chance of this happening now; but there is an element of disturbance and lawlessness in their separate and sectarian organization which in critical times might be dangerous, and is at all times injurious to political morality. Roman Catholicism among the Irish in Australia seems to be becoming less a Church than a political society. The priests are said not to be very strict about a man's morality, or how often or how seldom he goes to mass or confesses. If he pays his subscription to the priest or the new chapel when he is asked for it, and votes as he is told at the elections, he is a good Roman Catholic. It may almost be compared to the Vehmgericht, the Jacobin Society, the Evangelical Alliance, the Reform League, or the Trades' Unions. For all these have, or pretend to have, a germ of religion or *quasi*-religion in them which gives them their strength and coherence; and all have set up an authority unrecognised by the law, and have exercised influence chiefly by open or disguised intimidation.

Their ecclesiastical organization gives the Roman Catholics more political power than naturally belongs to them. A Squatter told me that even the maid-servants in his house up the country were called upon to pay a certain subscription, being assessed sometimes even as high as ten shillings, and woe to them if they refused! This is what is commonly called the voluntary system, for the law does not enforce payment, and its advocates point to the result in triumph. At the elections, if for any reason it is required of them, they obey orders, and vote as one man. Any 'private judgment' in such a case would be a grievous offence. A candidate at a coming election for a town in New South Wales was once asked for a subscription to a Roman Catholic charity. He promised a liberal donation, on condition that the money should not be used for proselytizing purposes. This, however, the applicant for the subscription refused to promise—in fact it was admitted that the money would be so employed—and so the candidate declined to give it. This was at Sydney.

A few days later he went to the town where the election was to be, at some distance up the country. He was unquestionably the popular candidate, and justly so, for he had been a benefactor to the neighbourhood. To his surprise one or two of his supporters came to express their regret that they could not vote for him, but assigned no reason. The election took place, and he was left behind in a small minority. The electors had obeyed ecclesiastical orders at the poll. They had not been, in the electioneering sense of the word, intimidated—had they not had the protection of the ballot, that infallible nostrum against intimidation?—and they had voted in accordance with their religious or ecclesiastical conscience, though against their individual inclination or judgment. Now they were free to express their own sympathies, which they did by seating the favourite but defeated candidate in a carriage by the side of the successful one, and making him share in the triumphal progress round the town.

This sort of influence is in its origin, if not in its essence, religious, and therefore out of reach of state interference. But its effect is political, and by producing a compact and powerful *imperium in imperio*, might become subversive of good government to a very serious extent, under a constitution in which a numerical majority, however composed, is all-powerful. If a third of the population, or thereabouts, choose to abdicate their individual wills and delegate their united strength to nobody knows who, bishop or conclave or priest, it may produce very serious political results.

People talk glibly enough about separation of Church and State as if it were a mere matter of pounds, shillings, and pence, a very simple connection capable of being made or dissolved in a moment by a vote or an Act of Parliament. But it sometimes happens that a man's Church allegiance and his State allegiance are much too intricately interwoven for any Act of any Parliament to separate. Where a man's religious creed (if he have any) centres, there generally will his political heart be also. The old Whig notion of a population holding all possible different beliefs and disbeliefs and yet remaining none the less cordially loyal to the State, may be a wholesome ideal for a statesman to have in his mind, but is impossible — even if desirable — to be really attained. The ex-Queen of Spain a short time ago sent a very handsome present of church-plate to the Roman Catholic Cathedral at Sydney. There was a great festival of the Roman Catholics on occasion of its being consecrated or placed in the Cathedral. It would have been interesting, if it had been possible, to analyse this *rapprochement* between Roman Catholic Spain and Roman Catholic Australia, and to discover how much was political and how much religious in it. Probably many an Irishman, if he had been asked, would have honestly answered that he believed the Queen of Spain to be the best and noblest of Sovereigns, and her government the most just, liberal, and enlightened in Europe; and if an occasion offered would vote or act in accordance with that idea, as with

K

a similar idea the Irish joined the Papal army to fight the King of Italy some years ago.

Fortunately, Australia is a long way from Rome, and it may be hoped that the ultramontane element in Romanism may give place gradually to a purer and more enlightened, if less strictly consistent and logical, secular patriotism. I believe there are some slight indications of this, here and there, alreddy. *Cælum non animum mutant qui trans mare currunt* is a maxim which does not apply so closely when the voyage is a very long one. But it may perhaps take a generation or two before any great change takes place, and in the meantime the element of divided allegiance is a dangerous one in the hands of the fanatical or the unscrupulously ambitious.

A few months ago the Roman Catholic chaplain of one of the Sydney convict establishments was found to be systematically inculcating Fenianism on his flock of gaol birds. He was dismissed. But from the outcry made in the House of Assembly and elsewhere about certain formalities or informalities in the manner of his dismissal, it was evident that the sympathies of many were with him. This is the more significant, from the fact that the priests in Ireland have, ostensibly at least, opposed the Fenian movement.

Not twenty years ago an Irishman who for a seditious libel had become acquainted with the inside of a gaol, and through a technical legal mistake had narrowly escaped a second conviction, emigrated to Melbourne. His reputation had preceded him, and he was received on landing with an ovation and a very handsome present of several thousand pounds. In responding he showed his sense of the course of conduct which had procured him this popularity, and announced with emphasis that he always had been and always should be a *rebel to the backbone*. Within a few years he was a member of the Ministry, and holding one of the most important offices in it. Being now comparatively wealthy and enjoying a very large pension for not very arduous services, he has become rather conservative than otherwise—does not altogether go with the present Government in the matter of the Lady Darling vote, for instance—and would fain have it forgotten, it is said, that he is pledged for life to ceaseless rebellion.

## XII.

### ARISTOCRACY AND KAKISTOCRACY.

The members of the Upper House or Legislative Council of New South Wales are nominated for life by the Governor, not elected, like those of Victoria and Tasmania, by a higher-class constituency. This plan was adopted by the framers of the Constitution with the intention of giving it a Conservative character. The effect has been the reverse of what was intended. A nominee of the Governor is generally in reality a nominee of the Ministry for the time being. Subject to his consent, it is in the power of the Ministry to swamp the Council by the creation of new members, and thus obtain a preponderating majority; and on at least one occasion this has been done. It is indeed understood that the Governor who gave his consent much regrets having done so, and it may be hoped that the experiment will not be repeated. But the authority of a legislative chamber cannot fail to be impaired by the bare possibility of such treatment. Under the most favourable circumstances, the Members, being nominated for having already attained a certain position in the colony, are not likely to be very young when appointed; and as they hold their seats for life, it is likely that there will generally be an unduly large proportion of old men. A Council so constituted, and having but little prestige of superior birth or education to support it, is not likely to be a match for a capricious and turbulent Lower House, borne on the flood-tide of present popularity, and ever ready to provide for present emergencies at the expense of the future. Hence it is not to be wondered at if it does not occupy so prominent a position relatively as the Victorian Council, which has lately so firmly and successfully opposed the unconstitutional proceedings of a Ministry supported by a large majority of the Lower House, and by a small majority of the population.

In answer to a question as to the character and composition of the Lower House, or Legislative Assembly, I was told that it was *now* no worse than that of Victoria. Probably this was about as much as could be said for it. The facts which I mentioned in a former letter concerning the Victorian Assembly may be an assistance in estimating the force of the comparison. I may add that since I wrote, one of its Members has been sentenced to a term of imprisonment for forgery, and the keeper of one of the most notoriously disreputable taverns in Melbourne has entered it, being chosen for an important district in preference to an opponent who is an old colonist, an educated gentleman, and a man of unquestionable ability and integrity.

One does not, however, hear in Sydney of the wholesale corruption, the taking of palpable 10*l.* notes, universally attributed to several legislators of the sister colony. The present Ministry of Mr. Martin and Mr. Parkes, in spite of some recent failures in finance, is generally described by reliable people as about the best since the existing Constitution came into force; and as the Opposition is weak, and contains few, if any, men of ability, the Government can do things pretty much in its own way. But other Administrations have been less powerful, and when they felt themselves tottering have, in order to prolong their lease of office a little longer, been sometimes by no means fastidious in the means they employed to obtain support. Different people were to be conciliated in different ways, and one of the results was the creation of a certain number of *Windmill Magistrates.* Lest the term *Windmill Magistrate* should be unintelligible to those who are not fully initiated into the mysteries of colonial democracy, perhaps I should explain that there have been persons aspiring, and not always in vain, to the honour of being magistrates, whose early education was not very comprehensive, and who, not being able to sign their names, were in the habit of affixing their mark × instead. The supposed resemblance of this mark to the sails of a windmill suggested the term.

Whatever be the cause or causes, the Legislative Assembly certainly is not held in much respect. It is in vain that its members strive to assert their importance by voting themselves free passes on the railways and a Members' Stand at the races. The leading Sydney paper, 'The Sydney Morning Herald,' has been publishing a series of articles, appearing two or three times a week, entitled 'The Collective Wisdom of New South Wales,' in which all the bad grammar, bad language, and extravagant and unbecoming behaviour of the Members, not mentioned in the reports of the debates, are chronicled and commented on. The following observations are from a leading article (not from one of the series I have alluded to) in the same paper,* which is as temperate and well conducted as any in Australia:—

'The specimens we have had of ribaldry and vituperation are, unhappily, too familiar with the Assembly, and even these hardly represent what is heard within the precincts of the Houses. We say, and with much regret, that there are members pretending to political leadership whose language would be a disgrace to a stable; who, when excited by drink or passion, pour out a stream of invective which is not merely blasphemous, but filthy. They have no hesitation to couple the names of persons with whom they have had more or less friendly intercourse, according as the changes of private interest or political sentiment may permit. . . . We believe that such language is rarely heard in British society of the present day. That it lingers in some parts of New South Wales is to be traced to causes which we shall not describe more specially, but which will, we hope, some day disappear. It is unfortunate when men who have been taught from their early youth to express themselves in a strain which becomes too natural by indulgence are in a position to propagate their example. . . . We can produce proofs to establish every syllable we say, namely, that the conspicuous men in the House, with one or two exceptions, have been for the last seven years accustomed to speak of each other in such terms as

* October 1, 1867.

gentlemen never apply, and excepting under the power of that mighty principle which conquers resentment, which gentlemen never forgive.'

Here is an extract from a debate in the Sydney Legislative Assembly :—*

'*Mr. M.* said that he only knew of one minister who ever attempted to make political capital out of religious differences.

'*An Hon. Member.*—Who?

'*Mr. M.*—The Colonial Secretary.

'*An Hon. Member*—" Shut up!"

'*Voices.*—" Boots," "laughing jackass," and other remarks, the application of which could only be seen by persons actually present, and the import of which it is hardly worth while to explain.

'*An Hon. Member.*—" How's your nose?"

'*Mr. M.*—Sir, I am sober; I hope you are.

'*An Hon. Member.*—" Who?"

'*Mr. M.*—Is the hon. member addressing me or addressing the chair?

'*Mr. F.*—The hon. member is addressing the "jackass."

'*An Hon. Member.*—Is that the "jackass?"

'*Mr. M.*—I have been told that there are liars and blackguards in this House, and I believe there are one or two.

'*Mr. P.*—I can see one now.

'*Mr. F.*—I move that the words be taken down.

'The words having been taken down by the clerk, and handed to the Chairman,

'*Mr. G.* read—" I see one now." (Great laughter.)

'*Mr. F.*—I have no hesitation in saying that the hon. member meant to say, and I do not think the hon. member is coward enough to deny—

* From *Hobart Town Mercury*, January 21, 1868, copied from the *Sydney Morning Herald.*

'*Mr. P.*—Does the hon. member accuse me of cowardice? Let him come outside and do it.

'*Mr. L.*—The hon. member does not accuse you of cowardice.

'*Mr. P.*—I know what he means. Let him come outside and say it.

'*Mr. H.* called attention to the presence of strangers in the House, and the reporters were again directed to withdraw.

'Up to our going to press, the House continued to sit with closed doors.'

As I write, the following account of a debate in the House, telegraphed to the Melbourne papers, is brought in :—

'The Opposition prevented a single item of the Estimates passing last night. During the debate a disgraceful scene took place. Mr. Forster insinuated that the Premier began his public career with perjury. Mr. Martin (the Premier) called Mr. Forster a liar and a blackguard repeatedly. The galleries were cleared, and the disorder lasted for two hours. Mr. Martin's words were taken down, but the Government members carried the previous question. Mr. Martin then apologized.'

Nor do members always confine their abusive language to each other. It sometimes happens that they bring charges against persons outside the House which those persons have no opportunity of answering, and for which, if false and libellous, no legal redress can be obtained, as the speakers are protected by privilege of Parliament. One of the very best and most valuable institutions of Sydney is the Grammar-school. Unfortunately there have been disputes about its management, and it has its enemies. One day a member rose in the House and charged one of the masters with habitually using expressions of the grossest blasphemy. The accused demanded of the School trustees an investigation. It was held. The charge broke down completely, being supported solely by the evidence of another master who in cross-examination was compelled to confess himself guilty of a string of deliberate falsehoods. Yet no retractation was made, no apology offered.

This state of things is not cheering. Men of by no means conservative or retrograde instincts will tell you sadly that it was not always so, that sixteen or seventeen years ago, in the days of mixed government, not only was the colony better governed, but it was in many respects in a sounder and healthier condition generally. The wealthy were not so wealthy, but neither were the poor so poor. There was work for all who wanted it, and at high wages. Now there is not a little pauperism and distress. Immigration was steadily increasing then; now it has almost ceased.

What is the cause? It is always dangerous to attempt to couple cause and effect in political matters, especially when events are so nearly contemporary. But there can be no doubt that the discovery of gold, if it has conferred wealth and brought advantages, has also brought serious temporary disadvantages which have not yet passed away. It would be hard to strike a balance between them. The population was greatly increased. But the whole framework of industry was put out of gear, and has hardly yet recovered the shock;

and the stream of immigration was not, as in Victoria, so great as to give an entirely new character to the colony and its population, and to build the framework afresh. It gave, too, a sudden and undue impulse to extreme democratic tendencies; and I think that the majority of well-informed men look upon the extreme democratic character of the existing constitution as amongst the principal causes of much of the misgovernment and corruption that exist. There are indeed few who ever say so publicly, and withstand Demos to his face; but at least one man, long the foremost champion of the anti-bureaucratic or popular party, to whom that party, in the days when they had real grievances to complain of, owed more than to anyone, has not shrunk from saying openly what he thinks or from deploring publicly the evil results of universal suffrage in the colony.*

It is bad enough to have bad legislation. But it is a much worse matter when those who originate it do so from weak or selfish motives, *knowing* that it is bad. In view of much that has been done, it is almost impossible to doubt that this has not infrequently been the case of late years in some of the Australian colonies, when we consider the comparatively high intellectual abilities of some of the leading statesmen, and consider also the notoriously low character of the various Legislative Assemblies with which they have had to deal. I believe the worst measures, amongst which the land-laws

---

\* See Mr. Wentworth's speech at the dinner to Sir John Young, reported in the *Times* in June 1868.

are pre-eminent, will in general be found to have been simply bids for popular support at the expense of common sense, common honour, and common patriotism, by men clinging selfishly to office for its own sake, and indifferent to the ultimate consequences of their policy.

In Tasmania things are not so bad. And that colony is at the present time singularly fortunate in possessing a Colonial Secretary whose name is a guarantee of fair and honourable dealing in the conduct of public affairs, who, unlike too many Australasian Colonial Secretaries, does not live with the love of office and the fear of Demos ever before his eyes. But the religion of Demos is not without a footing even there. I will give an instance, slight in itself, but significant. The Tasmanian climate does not admit the wine being made. Beer is made, but it is almost as dear as imported English beer. There is no cheap beverage, and as the climate (compared with that of England) is hot and dry, it would be a great boon, one would think, to be able to get the excellent, cheap light clarets and hocks of New South Wales. Unfortunately, there is an import duty of eight shillings a dozen, which, added to other charges, is, of course, simply prohibitory. Customs' revenue is sorely needed, as the returns have been falling off alarmingly for some years; and it is indisputable that a reduction of the duty on light wines would increase the amount of revenue from that source. But Demos does not drink light wine. His particular libation is rum. And so it is admitted that no one could venture to propose the reduction, because Demos, though his own pockets would gain by it, would raise an irresistible outcry at anyone getting wine cheap which he does not care for, unless at the same time the duty on rum were lowered, which the revenue cannot afford.

Great is the god Demos of the Australians! He is lavish in his rewards to his votaries while his favour lasts. But he is fickle, and must be humoured to the top of his bent, and worshipped with unswerving devotion. As long as statesmen bow at his shrine, so long will there be danger that Legislative Assemblies will be contemptible, individual members corrupt, magistrates incompetent, and the mass of the people tempted to lose reverence and regard for Queen, country, and law; so long also will successive ministries be compelled to go from bad to worse, to foster class prejudices and jealousies, to persistently misstate points at issue between them and their opponents, as the Victorian Ministers are doing at the elections now going on; so long also will their supporters not shrink even from exciting sedition by using language like the threat uttered the other day by the ministerialist candidate for North Gipps Land that 'the crack of the rifle may yet be heard beneath the windows of the Legislative Council.'

Some day or other, it may be, the question will be asked, Who destroyed a great empire? Who prematurely broke, or indolently suffered to be broken, a dominion that might have endured for generations? It will not, indeed, be easy to apportion the blame justly. Doubtless it would have been as practicable to dam up the river Hawkesbury in flood as to have simply defied the torrent of popular impulses in Australia. But all need not have been given up without a struggle. Something might have been saved, as by a little courage and skill a homestead here, an acre of corn there, is rescued from the flood. A Pitt, a Cromwell, even a Wellington with his simple straightforward love of good government in any form, would surely have done, or at least tried to do, something, whether popular or unpopular, to secure the 'carrying on of the Queen's government' firmly and honestly in her Australian colonies. But for the last sixteen years or so, since the old traditions of the conservative party have been abandoned, and it has been bidding for popular support by seeking to outdo its opponents in democratic concessions, the government of Australia by the Colonial Office has been gradually tending to become a simple 'cutting of straps,' and attempting, with very little regard to ultimate consequences, to please everybody, and fall in with the popular cry for the time being, whatever it might happen to be.

It is true that there were no aristocracies worthy of the name in the Australian colonies in whom a restraining power could be reposed (although in Victoria an aristocracy of mere wealth—perhaps the least desirable form of aristocracy—has by its representatives, the Legislative Council, just made a conspicuously steadfast and honourable stand against lawlessness and wrong). But surely some substantial power might have been left to the Governors. It would not have been difficult to have established some plan for so doing, with which the great majority of the colonists would have been well satisfied. It has been suggested to me by one who has had great colonial experience that the simple expedient of giving the Ministry for the time being *ex-officio* seats in the Legislative Assembly, would have had considerable effect, especially in the less populous colonies, in increasing the political influence of the Governor.

If this is not apparent at first sight, a little consideration will perhaps make it so. It must be remembered that in a colony where the population is comparatively small and public questions less numerous and intricate long parliamentary experience and skill in debate are not so absolutely essential to a Minister. It is quite possible that the fittest man to be Colonial Secretary or Treasurer may have had neither the opportunity nor the desire to obtain a seat in the Parliament; for the worthiest and fittest men have ordinarily little temptation to seek for one. Under the present system the Governor's choice of Ministers is practically confined to those who are in parliament. But if Ministers held seats *ex officio*, the Governor might choose anyone he liked and seat him at once. No doubt the Houses must so far ratify the Governor's choice as to give his Minister a majority, otherwise he could not carry his measures or remain in office; and this would suffice to prevent any specially unpopular man or policy from being put forward. But, in the first place, the mere addition of from three to seven votes in a House of from thirty to seventy members would be some slight addition to the strength of Government. This, however, is but a small matter. What is more important is that it would do much to prevent the growth, and to interfere with the organisation, of a merely factious Opposition. This sort of Opposition, based, as is generally the case in the colonial parliaments, on no sort of political principle, but cohering merely with the selfish and almost avowed object of seizing an opportunity for ousting Ministers and occupying their places, is a serious impediment to good and honest government. It is always on the watch to catch any passing breeze of popular clamour as a means of tripping up the Government, and the Government is in self-defence obliged to be equally amenable and subservient. When the Administration appears strong, and seems likely to remain in, the Members of the House crowd their ranks for the sake of the loaves and fishes; and the Opposition is left scarcely strong enough to exercise legitimate control over the expenditure. But when the loaves and fishes are nearly all gone, and especially if there is any suspicion of ministerial insecurity, there comes a serious defection from their supporters. Thus the Opposition may be composed chiefly of disappointed deserters from the other side, and in a small colony may sometimes contain scarcely a single man of weight or ability, or who is in any way fitted to be entrusted with office. Yet it is worth while for them to persist and to watch their opportunities, for sooner or later every Ministry must fall, and under the present system the Governor has no choice but to send for the leader of Opposition, or, in the absence of anyone entitled to be so considered, for the mover of the motion the success of which has caused the crisis. Now the effect of giving *ex-officio* seats to Ministers would be this. The knowledge that the Governor might, if he thought fit, make his next selection of advisers from outside Parliament altogether, would make the objects pursued by a merely factious Opposition too uncertain of attainment to be worth contending for with such persistence. The prospect of being possibly left out in the cold altogether would weaken their cohesion and diminish their strength; while to a corresponding extent the Government would be strengthened, and would be better enabled to dispense with those means of conciliating their supporters which are so fertile a source of one-sided class-legislation and of corruption.

In its Colonial Governors, England possesses a body of tried and faithful servants in whom it may well place confidence. Many of them have had experience and training from their youth upwards in the work of governing. The Home Government can select them from any profession; it can appoint them on the simple ground of fitness without any arbitrary or technical qualification; it can recall them at its pleasure. Gentlemen by birth and education, many of them picked men from the army or navy (almost the only callings in modern times where men learn to obey, and therefore the fittest for learning to command), impartial upon the petty local questions which vex colonial statesmen, they are (with an exception here and there) eminently well qualified for governing new and unsettled communities, and in three cases out of four infinitely superior in ability, as in everything else, to the Ministers whose advice they are now obliged to follow. Of course, there have been exceptions, and because of them no one would for a moment wish to see restored the almost absolute power which Governors possessed in the very early days when they had no one to rule over but soldiers and convicts. But surely it was a fatal mistake by a stroke of the pen to limit the functions of the not unworthy successors of the Phillipses, the Collinses, and the Bourkes, to holding levées and giving balls.

Sir Charles Hotham, when Governor of Victoria, foreseeing what would happen, when some modifications of the Constitution were sent home for ratification, wrote a despatch pointing out the powerless condition to which his authority was being reduced. It was not perhaps altogether a logical or judicious despatch. Sir Charles Hotham was a sailor, without any previous experience in government, promoted from the quarter-deck to a most difficult and responsible position, at a most critical time; and it was not surprising if he had not thoroughly mastered the intricate clauses of a Constitution Act. But if Lord John Russell (then at the Colonial Office) had wished to discredit the Queen's Representative, he could hardly have done it more effectually than he did by publishing the despatch, to be a butt (which at that time, from its Conservative tone, it was sure to be) for the vituperation of the colonial press.* Up to this time the Colonial Governors had found it impossible to obtain from the Colonial Office at home even an outline of the course they were to pursue with reference to the new Constitutions. No instructions whatever were vouchsafed in answer to their enquiries. But at last the Secretary for the Colonies had spoken out. There was a significance about the publication of this despatch which could not be mistaken. Sir Charles Hotham died a few months afterwards, worn out by overwork, anxiety, and hostility on all sides. And since that time every Governor in a constitutional colony knows that his office is all but a cipher, and that the Colonial Office is content to have it so.

I have known a Governor ask his Ministers for a simple Return, for the information of the Home Government, for three years, without succeeding in obtaining it. Even their social power is curtailed. Marks of distinction, instead of being conferred according to their recommendation, are given at haphazard, often to the most unfit recipients. Perhaps as effectual and desirable a means, as far as it goes, of preserving a close union and sympathy between the colonists and the old country would be to induce the sons of colonists to serve in the British Army and Navy. It was accordingly suggested that Governors should have the power of recommending for a certain number of com-

* See *Argus* of July 26, 1855.

missions. The Home Government approved, and expressed its approval by according to each of the Australian Governors the astonishing privilege of presenting to *one* cadetship in the Navy *once in three years*!

## XIII.

### MOTHER AND DAUGHTER.

There exists in England a school of politicians, or economists, which considers it desirable that the Australasian colonies should at once, or before long, be cast loose from the Mother-country. There are doubtless some amongst the colonists who are of the same opinion; but I believe that they are very few in number, and that it will be England's fault, more than that of her colonies, if—in our day at least—the Empire is broken up.

Of course it is easy to point to mistakes made by the Home Government in the old days when it had all the power and responsibility in its own hands. And since self-government has been accorded to the colonies, faults of a different kind have been committed on both sides. Latterly, and while Administrations in England have been displacing each other so rapidly, and throwing out feelers for all the support they could get, there has been an increasing disposition to yield indolently to every passing cry of the hour with too little regard to ultimate results, and sometimes to the discouragement of the most loyal, temperate, and far-seeing among the colonists. On the other hand, the colonists have now and then shown themselves eager to claim the privileges without bearing the responsibilities of Englishmen.

Chief amongst vexed questions, in old times, was that of transportation. For many years there was frequent vacillation in the policy of the Home Government. Each new Head of the Colonial Office had his own plan to carry out, and the consequence was either to flood the colonies with convicts, or else to stop the supply too abruptly. One unfortunately expressed despatch was misunderstood, and gave rise, not unnaturally, to a charge of breach of faith with the inhabitants of Van Diemen's Land.* The excessive and unreasonable number of convicts which had been poured in upon them gave the Tasmanians just cause for protesting as they did (not unanimously indeed, but by a large majority) against the continuance of transportation in any form to their own shores. But, on the other hand, it gave the Victorians no excuse for so unreasonable a demand, as that it should cease thenceforward to all Australia, lest a stray convict should escape now and then to their own colony. Western Australia, for instance, has an impassable desert between it and any other colony, and communication by sea is very infrequent; and its free inhabitants, like the free inhabitants of most of the other colonies in their early stages of development, have been asking

* See Lord Grey's *Colonial Policy of the Administration of Lord J. Russell*, vol. ii. p. 18. The average annual number of convicts sent to Van Diemen's Land, from 1840 to 1845, was no less than 3,527 annually (see p. 5).

for convicts as a boon. And there is still an enormous amount of coast-line and territory unsettled, where it is very probable that convicts may, at some future time, be an advantage. It is unreasonable that colonies should claim to draw from the able-bodied and politically untainted population of the Mother-country just as they choose; that they should have the power to bribe them out, or discourage their coming, just as it happens to suit their ideas of what will benefit themselves; and yet that they should exclaim against taking at least their share of the criminally-disposed, or even pauper, part, which their vast extent of country renders comparatively innocuous, and for the amelioration of whose condition it affords such advantages. It is as unreasonable and selfish and 'colonial' (to use the word in the bad sense which it sometimes bears in Australia), as if Torquay or Madeira were to refuse to admit consumptive patients among their visitors, or Belgravia object to afford a site to St. George's Hospital.

If the wishes or demands of the colonists were in old times treated with too little consideration, the reaction has been excessive. When the colonies were given up under their new Constitutions, almost without reserve, each to its own local government, the arrangement under which it was effected was a most one-sided one. In its origin Australia, taken as a whole, is essentially a Crown settlement. But for Captain Cook, a king's officer sailing in a king's ship, and but for transportation, which followed soon after, it might not have held an Englishman till half a century later; or it might have been a French possession, as the Middle Island of New Zealand was within six hours of being. Phillip, Hunter, Collins, Flinders, Bass, the early heroes and discoverers of Australia, were king's officers, military or naval. Millions from the Imperial treasury were spent in wharves, lighthouses, roads, bridges, public buildings. With this money, and by convict labour, was the country made habitable and valuable. Even Victoria, though no convicts ever were sent direct to Port Phillip, was colonised from New South Wales and Van Diemen's Land, and it was by convict shepherds that it was first made productive and opened up—of which the discovery of gold was the consequence. All the public works, and the whole of the territory of each colony, occupied or unoccupied, surveyed or unsurveyed, were surrendered as a free gift. I say as a gift; for that a quarter or half a million of inhabitants should assert an exclusive claim to millions of acres never utilised and hardly explored, would be about as unreasonable as was John Batman's claim to possess all the shores of Port Phillip because he was the first to pitch his tent there. What the value of the Crown lands thus given up may amount to in fifty or a hundred years it is impossible to give the wildest guess, but at any rate it will be measured by hundreds of millions. And for all this the only obligation given in return was the annual charge of the Civil List—a mere payment to the Governor and his staff. And even this has sometimes been grudged.

The payment to the Governor of Victoria was reduced, and an attempt has lately been made to reduce that to the Governor of Tasmania, with as much reason as if half the price of a horse were to be claimed back by the buyer years after it had been bought.

Nor was any pledge asked or given that Australian markets should be kept open to English manufactures. The result already has been that one colony after another has been establishing and increasing protective duties, which as respects some articles are almost prohibitory to English goods. The only stipulation made was that duties charged to England should be charged equally to all the world, so as to let in English manufactures on the same terms with foreign and those from other colonies. Even this it is now sought to have relaxed, so as to establish intercolonial free-trade, in which the Mother-country is not to be admitted to share.

But there is no use in dwelling too long on past mistakes. As to the future, I must confess myself unable to understand how any Englishman could fail to feel it as a deep disgrace, if, unsolicited and for the sake of any real or imaginary commercial advantage, or from sheer laziness and unwillingness to bear an honourable responsibility, we were to renounce our inheritance in our colonies. Great as the loss would be to us, to them it would assuredly be far greater in every respect. Without the protection of a strong naval Power they would be simply at the mercy of the first powerful fleet and army which France, Russia, or the United States might send to take possession of them. The smallness of the population, the extent of coast, and the wide distances between the few large towns, would make defence, however resolute, against any considerable force altogether unavailing. The gold-mines of Ballarat and Bendigo and the copper-mines of Burra-burra are as rich and tempting to an invader as anything in Siberia or Persia, or in Algeria or Mexico.

No doubt it is possible that a Federation or union of some kind might be devised, not under the British Crown, but having an alliance offensive and defensive with it. But it is difficult to conceive of any such which would last. If Australia were to enter into distinct diplomatic relations with other Powers, European or other, it would soon become impossible for us to take up their quarrels, or for them to take up ours. As their union would not be very close, their policy would not be likely to be a very steady or consistent one.

For the climate of different parts of the continent differs widely, the productions are increasingly different; hence, and from many other causes, men's habits, ideas, and tastes tend to divergence rather than to convergence. Already there are occasional manifestations of antagonism between some of the different colonies, which, though slight and comparatively harmless under a common but separate allegiance, might become more serious between members of a Federation. It was a good joke, and not an ill-timed one under the circumstances, for Melbourne, before Victoria was a separate colony, to elect Lord Grey as its representative to the House of Assembly at Sydney, by way of a hint that it really was time for them to be a colony by themselves. But it is a little too much, now that it has been all settled to their satisfaction years ago, and Melbourne has long since shot ahead of Sydney in population and importance, to keep ' Separation-day ' as a general holiday and day of rejoicing, as if New South Wales were the one thing on earth from which they were thankful for deliverance. Such manifestations do not bode well for future union.

If anyone wishes to form a conception of the narrowing and deteriorating influences which must exist, even under the present or the most favourable circumstances, in a colony, for instance, of the size of Tasmania, let him imagine the inhabitants of any English provincial town amounting to nearly a hundred thousand, spread over a country as big as Ireland, and encircled by a wall through which there can only be communication perhaps twice a week with two or three neighbouring provincial towns, and only once a month with the rest of the world, from which, too, all communications must wait seven weeks till they are delivered. Would Nottingham or Bristol, or even Birmingham or Manchester, be likely to contribute much to the enlightenment of mankind under such circumstances? People in England do not realise what drops in the ocean of territory the Australian populations are. The wonder rather is how *much* intellectual energy there is, and how favourably the population of many of the colonies would compare with that of many manufacturing towns at home. But of those who now go to Australia from England, an overwhelming proportion are from the labouring or comparatively unlearned classes. The proportion of clergymen, barristers, and university men who go out now is very insignificant compared with what it once was, and anything which caused it to diminish still more would be a misfortune. Local interests and local connections make it difficult for an emigrant from England any longer to compete in the race with the colonial-born in any profession with much chance of success. It was my good fortune to be present at a gathering at Melbourne of all old Oxford and Cambridge men who could be collected. There were about thirty present. They included the Governor, the Bishop, two or three leading politicians of the Opposition—the rest chiefly professors, clergymen, barristers, squatters, or doctors. Considering its small number it was a remarkably influential group. But I was struck with the regretful but unhesitating opinion expressed, that the number was likely to diminish rather than to increase, especially in the ranks of the clergy. In all the professions this is to be regretted, and amongst the clergy more particularly, because it is upon them as a class that any narrowness or incompleteness of education tells with most fatal effect. There are indeed both at Melbourne and at Sydney, Universities, which as far as I could judge are excellently managed and liberally supported, and unquestionably contain professors of the very first rank of ability. But it is impossible for any colonial university, in the midst of a small society in which almost all interests are swamped in the overwhelming one of commerce, to carry education to a very high point. A few people who are particularly anxious for a good education for their sons, send them home for five or six years; but most are content with a colonial university for them, and often remove them when they are still almost boys.

There are many causes to account for the diminishing supply of well-educated clergymen from home. A clergyman's position in a colony is very different from what it is in England. For liberty and subsistence he is more at the mercy of others. To a certain extent (to what extent I do not know) there are fixed stipends attached to parochial cures, but in the absence of a regularly established and endowed Church, the clergy are likely to be much more than in England dependent for subsistence upon their popularity. Many high-minded clergymen are naturally reluctant to put themselves in a position where their very bread may depend upon their catering successfully for the tastes of their parishioners, and where they would be constantly under the temptation to devote their energies merely or chiefly to exciting or amusing their hearers once a week. The fixed annual grants originally given out of the State-funds to the clergy are being gradually withdrawn, either ceasing with the lives of the present holders, or having been commuted for a lump sum paid to a trust-fund. In one township in New South Wales it was satisfactory to find that the inhabitants had insured the life of the present incumbent, with whom 'State-aid' (as it is called) was to cease, and were paying the annual premiums, so as at his death to have a sum to invest in trust for his successors—to endow a living, in fact.

Happily for its peace, representatives of the extreme religious parties of the Church are rare in Australia. An underpaid and overworked clergy has not either time or money to spare for imitating Roman Catholic vestments or Exeter Hall invective. The Scotch often join in helping to build an English church, and are regular attendants upon its services. Hence, fortunately, it has seldom if ever been necessary to ascertain what the exact legal status of a clergyman of the Church of England in the various colonies is—how, for instance, and for what, and by whom he is removeable—and I never could get any very clear account of it. I believe it is at the present time somewhat undefined and uncertain. Ecclesiastical synods are held from time to time, and (especially at Sydney) seem to do a good deal of business, and to be possessed of considerable responsibility and power. But in general the bishop of each diocese appoints the clergy to their cures, and has, I believe, the absolute power of removing or suspending them. The bishops are naturally unwilling to exercise this last power except for flagrant moral offences, and for causes in which they and the parishioners interested concur. But it is a power so obviously liable to abuse that the right of appeal from it seems indispensable.

All these difficulties and evils are likely to be increased by separation from the Mother-Church at home. In Victoria the clergy almost without a dissentient voice subscribed to the earnest protest which was sent to England against any scheme of Church separation. Religious and ecclesiastical isolation is worse than secular in the same degree that religious and ecclesiastical life has a greater tendency than secular to narrowness and intensity. I cannot but think that the separation of the different colonial churches from the English Church would be a wilful removal of a precious safeguard against religious ignorance, bigotry, and intolerance, and that the substitution of the final authority of local synods or bishops or parish-vestries for that of the wide but definite limits of the Articles, interpreted by that bulwark of the liberty of the English clergy, the Judicial Committee of the Privy Council, would be, not to give liberty, but to bind on the clergy heavy fetters and grievous to be borne.

I cannot conceive it possible, as some do, that political and ecclesiastical separation could fail to promote isolation of ideas, to diminish the flow of intercourse and sympathy, and to breed jealousies and heartburnings between the new country and the old. The Mails might go as often, ships and steamers be as numerous, and commerce carried on as before. But if commercial intercourse unites countries in the bonds of peace and mutual interests, it also, when pushed too eagerly and too exclusively, may rouse the spirit of covetousness, selfishness, jealousy, and division. Those who have leaned upon commerce as a sufficient means of bringing peace and good-will upon earth have, sooner or later, found that they have been leaning on a broken reed. A glance at Australia will show how little 'well-established and enlightened commercial principles' are carried out by those who fancy they can gain a temporary pecuniary advantage by repudiating them.

That the attachment to the Old Country and to the Crown is strong, is abundantly evident everywhere. It is stronger of course with the English-born than the native-born, and hence it is particularly observable in Victoria. It is seldom that even the most contemptible demagogues venture to trifle with it. Amongst other small items of English news, the Mail once brought word that a leading Oxford Professor was going to leave England and settle in America. Such a thing would scarcely be noticed in an English newspaper, but it was thought worthy of being announced amongst the items of intelligence telegraphed from Adelaide in advance of the mail-steamer, and was alluded to by the leading Melbourne paper with a shout of satisfaction. Yet the paper had no complaint to make of him except one. He had made himself conspicuous amongst those who have declared themselves in favour of turning the colonies adrift.

It is in the nature of things almost inevitable that the second generation of a colony should be inferior to the first. The struggles and hardships which pioneer settlers have to encounter constitute a discipline and confer an experience such as scarcely any other life can afford, and are a great contrast to the routine life and physical comforts to which the next generation succeeds. These old colonists, too, have had an old-world training in addition to the experience of the new. They know well how much they owe to having been born and bred amongst the historic monuments and associations of the old country of their forefathers, and that it is not mere foolish sentiment that binds them to it. None feel so keenly how real and not sentimental is the loss which their children suffer by being removed from and in part deprived of them. None regret so bitterly the relaxing and severing of bond after bond, or (if it were in danger) would cling so closely to the last but strongest bond of all—allegiance to the English Throne.

## XIV.

### HOME AGAIN.

The voyage home from Australia is a less easy and pleasant one than the voyage out. Owing to the prevalence of strong westerly winds for the greater part of the year in the South Pacific and Southern Indian Ocean, homeward-bound ships almost invariably sail eastward round Cape Horn, though the distance that way is greater, instead of westwards by the Cape of Good Hope. In rounding Cape Horn they must go to at least 56° south, and these latitudes have a disagreeable reputation for heavy gales, fogs, icebergs, and intense cold. To get amongst the icebergs in a fog, and with half a gale of wind blowing, is a very serious business indeed; and in spite of the utmost precaution many good ships have had hairbreadth escapes in this part of the voyage. During January, February, and March, indeed, the westerly winds are not so regular—old Horsburgh noted this fact as much as fifty years ago—and a Melbourne ship now and then manages to get round Cape Leeuwin and to the Cape of Good Hope. And ships sailing from Adelaide, being already so far to the west, attempt this course at all times of year, so that you may get a passage home by the Cape by sailing from hence. But it is a tedious voyage at best. A hundred days is a quicker voyage this way than eighty days by Cape Horn.

Then there is the way home by New Zealand and Panama, which takes about eight weeks from Melbourne. And, lastly, there are the Peninsular and Oriental Company's mail-steamers, which are in correspondence with the Calcutta and China mail-steamers, which they meet at Galle; and this is the quickest, the most interesting, and, from October to April, the pleasantest way of going.

Punctually to the hour the anchor of the trim little *Bombay* is got up. A Peninsular and Oriental steamer scorns the contact, it seems, of almost any wharf but that of her own native Southampton, and waits with proper dignity in mid-harbour to take in her passengers not only at Melbourne, but even at Sydney, the starting-place of her voyage. So there is no shore-tackle to be loosed. In an instant the powerful screw is revolving, making the whole ship quiver and vibrate, the water in the glasses spirt up and spill, and the passengers at the saloon-table shake and nod over their luncheon as though they had the palsy. For the last time we pass through Port Phillip Heads, and steer straight across the Australian Bight.

One more glimpse of the new Southern world we have before striking straight across the Indian Ocean to the old Oriental one. At sunset about five days after leaving Melbourne the land is in sight again, and soon after the distant glimmer of the lighthouse which stands on a little rocky island at the mouth of King George's Sound. In a few hours we enter the Sound, a large harbour or bay, land-locked except to the south and south-east, embraced by a confusion of long irregular promontories and islands between which the eye cannot distinguish, and bare of tree or house to disturb their undulating outline. So white they look in the moonlight, that they might be bare chalk hills, and even by daylight it is difficult to make out that it is only pure white sand which covers them. A few lights on shore ahead of us are the only sign of life. Even the pilot seems to be asleep, for we have to burn blue-lights and rockets to summon him as we steam on at half-speed. At last he comes on board, looking very sleepy; we enter the inner harbour, the anchor drops, and the twelve hours' work of coaling is at once begun, and goes on continuously throughout the night.

Daylight reveals that in all the great natural harbour there is only one sea-going vessel, the Adelaide packet, which has come to meet us. There are still three or four hours left, and we land in one of the boats on the pretty sandy shore, and make our way through low scrub towards the settlement. The flowers are lovely, especially a large brilliant red bottle-brush, and a handsome white flower growing on a bush with slimy sticky leaves, which is the fatal poison-plant, or one of them, which has been so injurious to Western Australia, by poisoning the sheep and making the land valueless for grazing. As for Albany, the settlement, it is a pleasant, cosy little village of wooden houses, with three or four superior habitations for the Government officials and the Peninsular and Oriental agent; and considering that it is on a splendid harbour, and situated in the extreme corner of a great continent, it is about as quiet, dull, lifeless, and unprogressive a place as can well be conceived. For what is there to be done there? The climate is said to be particularly charming, but the soil is so poor and sandy that even the few hundred inhabitants can scarcely grow food for their own wants. There is an establishment of convicts here, and they are to be seen doing such work as can be found for them; and in one respect it is a good place for them, for there is little chance of their escaping. From the top of a hill we could see to a great distance inland, but there is scarcely a sign of habitation or even a large tree to be seen. The nearest station is fifty miles off, and Perth, the only considerable town, two hundred and fifty. The road to it is plainly visible for miles and miles, stretching straight across the plain. The native black-fellows frequent the place, and are to be seen more in their original condition here than in most other parts of Australia—repulsive-looking, dark-brown figures, their hair and bodies smeared with grease, boomerangs and spears in their hands, and opossum skins sewn together hung on them as on a clothes-horse, and making a poor apology for clothing.

It is hard to understand how the settlement contrived

to exist at all before the days when the Peninsular and Oriental steamers made it a coaling-station, and a place for meeting the Adelaide steamer. But it is an old settlement, as I was reminded in a very unexpected and startling way by an object that I should as soon have expected to see in Belgrave Square as there—a common parish *Stocks*, in perfect repair!

But at noon the *Bombay's* gun booms over the dead silence of the sunny landscape, as a signal to go on board again, and we take our last look at Australia. In the *Bombay* one seems to be already almost in India. The ship's company are a medley of races from Europe, Asia, and Africa. The officers of course, and the quartermasters, and a few more, are English. But the great majority are black or bronze-coloured. The captain has a boat's crew of nine fine sailor-like Malays, who cannot speak a word of English. Amongst the stewards in the saloon are two or three pure African negroes, and very good servants they are. The firemen and stokers are long, lean, gaunt, black Abyssinians. The rest of the crew is perhaps made up of Lascars or other natives of India, small feeble-looking men, whom one sees eating their meagre fare of rice and curry, half a dozen of them squatting on the deck round a bowl of it, into which they dip their long bony fingers. They have to make up by their numbers for their want of muscle. To see a dozen of them pulling at a rope you would think each of them was afraid of breaking it. It is a sight to see all the crew mustered on Sunday morning for inspection on the after-deck, ranged in order according to their different departments, and each dressed in his cleanest and best. Side by side with the English sailor's dress are turbans, and tunics of green, red, or yellow silk, and bracelets, and all the brilliant colours of Oriental costume. Yet all this heterogeneous crew is in perfect discipline. The orderliness, cleanliness, and smartness of the decks, and of everything on board, is a great contrast to the ordinary condition of a merchant ship, and comes very near to that of a man-of-war.

It is about a fortnight's run from King George's Sound to Galle. Every day the heat sensibly increases. It is hotter, it seems, in the Indian Ocean than on the Atlantic. One day the thermometer on deck, with a double awning above, stands at 91°, and I cannot discover that there is any artificial heat to affect it. In the cabin it is about 87°, but with the ports open, and a wind-sail to direct a current of air in upon the berths, sleep is not difficult. The Lascars in their scanty linen clothing, who have been huddling miserably round the funnel for warmth, now squat on the deck and play at cards, flinging them down with great animation when their turn comes to play; but they still keep near the funnel as a pleasant friend and neighbour. Down the stoke-hole, where the Abyssinian firemen feed the fire, the thermometer is said to stand at 156°—I did not go down to try—and one of the long gaunt black figures, with scarcely a rag of clothing on and shining with moisture emerges to the upper regions from time to time, and a bucket of water is thrown over him to revive him. The mysterious little pulley-wheels near the saloon ceiling are explained now; for punkahs are put up, and little bronze-faced boys in white shirts and trousers squat in pretty attitudes, exactly like the figures which support French lamps, and pull away patiently at the punkah-strings to make the heat more tolerable for those who are sitting at table. The flying-fish know their latitude to a degree, and make their appearance as soon as the tropic is entered. But they are not so numerous as in the Atlantic, or else the steamer scares them away. One flying higher than usual and losing its presence of mind strikes one of the ship's officers on the head, nearly knocking him off the bridge where he was walking, and breaking its own head with the force of the shock. Day by day the sunsets grow more gorgeous, and the crimson and purple lights on the calm oily water more dreamily beautiful. The concavity of the crescent moon turns more and more upwards till it is cup-like and horizontal. The Great Bear reappears, but in humble fashion close to the horizon, and draggling his poor dear tail in the water as if half ashamed, and languishing in these hot southern latitudes. At last a penknife stuck in the bulwarks at noon casts no shadow; for we are leaving the Southern Hemisphere.

One morning the screw has stopped, and the sun rises, and the morning mist lifts, to show us an open bay into which the surf dashes unrestrained, and which is fringed on one side with a thick wood of cocoa-nut palms and tropical undergrowth, with here and there a bungalow or a little hut, while on the other side of the bay a road runs along the base of stone-faced ramparts covered with the freshest, greenest turf, and leads up to a seventeenth-century gateway, by which a crowd of people are passing in and out. Within the walls are the red and purple tiled roofs, and strong tropical lights and shadows of Galle. It is an exquisite scene to wake up to from the formless solitude of mid-ocean. Paddling round about the vessel are swarms of small craft, barge-like boats, and long picturesque canoes scarcely more than a foot wide, made of a hollowed tree, and balanced on the tossing swell by a small beam fastened parallel to them by outriggers six or eight feet long and resting on the water. They are manned by natives vociferously vending newspapers, fruit, or trinkets, or bargaining to take passengers ashore.

Ashore all go as soon as possible, and through the gateway, and up a street shaded by a green avenue, till the great Oriental Hotel is reached, the large broad verandah of which is crowded with people in all the strange costumes and head-gear of Anglo-Indians; talking, flirting, smoking, eating, drinking, bargaining, and abusing the (at this time of year) more than Indian heat. They are passengers going to, or returning from, India and China. For Galle is the Rugby Junction of Anglo-Asiatic traffic, where the China and Australia steamers disgorge their passengers into the larger vessel from Calcutta and Madras—many rills flowing into one stream—and there are often a couple of days to be spent here waiting—days inexpressibly full of interest and enjoyment to those to whom the scenes of India and of the tropics are new and unfamiliar.

The streets are full of natives, clothed or half-clothed in white or coloured cotton dress. The driver of your hired carriage who sits close in front of you is perhaps bare to the waist; but the dark-brown colour of his skin prevents you from being keenly alive to the fact, and you are not much impressed with any deficiency in his apparel. Men as well as women wear their black hair long and tied in a knot, or confined by tortoiseshell combs. Indeed the general appearance of men and women is so much alike that at first sight one is almost puzzled to distinguish them. A lady lately arrived at Galle, talking to a friend who had been much in her house and knew all about her establishment, happened to mention her ayah. The friend expressed surprise, as he did not know she had an ayah; and after explanation, and summoning the servant in question, she was made aware that her servant was a man, and had never pretended to be anything else, though he had been acting as nurse, and washing and dressing the baby for a week or two.

Crowding round the verandah of the hotel is a host of importunate vendors of tortoiseshell, baskets, ivory boxes, and jewellery. As regards jewellery there is ample scope for their roguery, which is without limit. A fellow will ask you fourteen pounds for what he calls a real sapphire ring, and gladly let you have it, after a little bargaining, for two shillings. Europeans take unblushing rascality of this sort as a matter of course, and treat it, not with indignation, but with contempt. Even in a few hours one can understand a little why the natives are so often treated by Europeans much in the way that a good-natured man treats a useful dog.

The hotel is a great building, with the bedrooms for greater coolness separated by partitions reaching only part of the way to the ceiling, so that a word or a snore is sometimes audible in every room from one end to the other of the long corridor; and many are the reproaches, expletives, bolsters, boots, and other missiles, which are flung over the partition at anyone who offends in this latter particular. In some of the private houses the doors are for the same reason made so as to come within a foot of the ground, and consequently when anyone is coming into the room there is ample time and opportunity for inspecting his or her feet, &c. before any other part of the person is visible.

The heat does not admit of much going about in the middle of the day; but towards evening you can drive beyond town and suburbs, and see the palms on each side bending over the road, and the rich swampy soil teeming with rank vegetation, and feast your senses on the often-described wonders of a tropical climate. Beautiful as it is, it is not to be compared for beauty (one is told) with the interior. And there is no time or opportunity for seeing that, for punctual to its day the great black hull of the steamer from Calcutta and Madras, which is to pick up all the passengers for Suez;

rounds the point and enters the bay, and by daybreak next morning she is off again.

A huge monster she is of two thousand six hundred tons or thereabouts, with a charming long flush deck from bows to stern of immense length. She is cramfull; for it is the end of March, and all Indians who can get away—officers, civilians, invalids, and young children—are on their way home before the hot season sets in. Some cabins have been reserved for passengers waiting at Galle, and we from Australia are a not very welcome addition to the already large number, and are probably set down as at best successful diggers, and as most likely holders of tickets-of-leave. But with or without tickets-of-leave we soon shake down, and get on pretty well with each other, for there is no room for quarrelling. There are some five hundred human beings on board, of whom more than half are passengers, and of these above fifty are children. They are pale, sickly, quiet little beings, these children, or one does not know how the ship would hold them, for they are under little or no control. Often half a dozen or more have been confided to the care of one invalid lady, who has about enough to do to take care of herself. As for the ayahs, of whom there are plenty, they have not a shadow of authority over their charges, and submit as a matter of course to thumps and abuse in answer to their feeble threats and entreaties.

It is worth while to stroll over the ship about midnight, when everyone has settled down for the night.

The season is not yet advanced and hot enough to oblige everyone to sleep on deck, but on the after-deck under the awning are perhaps twenty men-passengers asleep—some on mattresses brought up from their cabins, others on the benches or on cane lounging-chairs. Forward, near the funnel and galley and on the forecastle, the bright moonlight shines upon bodies lying as thick and as motionless as on a battle-field after a battle—some wrapped head and all in their garments of white linen or coarse cloth, some in their natural bare black to the waist, some huddled together, head to feet, in groups, and some alone, and all without the slightest regard to whether they are in the gangway or not. In the saloon, on the tables, or on the narrow benches, with one leg on the table to keep them from rolling off, lie white-shirted and white-trousered stewards; and on the floor at their mistresses' cabin-doors are prostrate ayahs, so exactly in the way that in the half-light one almost has to feel for them to avoid treading on them in passing. On the lockers in the stern are a few children and an ayah or two; but the head-quarters of the children are down below on the lower-deck, where they are laid out by dozens on the table, on cushions, shawls, and anything that comes to hand, while over them the punkah, its strings connected with the engines, fans the air steadily the whole night through. And all seem to sleep peacefully and even comfortably each after his fashion, for the north-east monsoon is just dying away, there is not a wave to stir the ship, and every port and scuttle to within two or three feet of the water-line is open to admit the air.

We carry on the monsoon till Cape Guardafui is in sight; then comes a strong south-east breeze heavy with moisture blowing up the gulf, and on the morning but one after, the rising sun lights up brilliantly the red and yellow mountains which stretch across the little peninsula of Aden, rising up behind it in high peaks and ridges abrupt and sharp and serrated like the Dolomite mountains of the Tyrol. And in an hour or two the *Tarus* drops her anchor within a quarter of a mile of the shore, among steamers and ships of war and transports on their way to Annesley Bay to feed the Abyssinian Expedition, now near its goal at Magdala.

Like King George's Sound, Aden is an isolated corner of a continent, cut off by deserts from land-communication with the outer world of civilization, and important only as a refuge or coaling-station for shipping. Wild tribes of Bedouins are the only inhabitants of the deserts which bound the peninsula, and for some years after our occupation of it they made repeated attacks upon us; and strong fortifications, garrisoned chiefly by Bombay sepoy regiments, now guard the small space where it is possible to penetrate the strong natural defence of the mountains.

And the impression of strange wild primeval desolation is increased as we land. Moist as is the air in the gulf, the atmosphere of Aden itself is as dry as can be conceived, and tempts one, protected by a green veil and an umbrella, to ride or walk, or even run, in spite of the fierce sun which blazes out of the unclouded sky. Scarcely a morsel of vegetation, not a blade of grass is to be seen, only at rare intervals in the sand a leafless shrub. For at Aden not a drop of rain falls often for years in succession, though the mountain-peak not four miles from the harbour is capped with cloud. Water is supplied chiefly by distillation from the sea, and also from huge tanks. We drive to see them, passing strings of camels, and tall, dirty, melancholy, scowling Arabs, and a wretched Arab village of huts of mud and straw like a warren of ill-instructed rabbits, and turn up a hill through fortifications and covered ways hewn in the rock, where white-coated sepoy sentinels stand on guard, and down on the other side to the cantonments and to the Arab town of Aden itself, for where we landed is not Aden proper but the Bunder or port. They are a strange memorial of the past, those tanks. They are hewn out of the solid rock one above another in a steep gulley of the cloud-capt mountain, from whence at long intervals torrents of water pour down and fill them. Tradition assigns them an origin anterior to the time of Abraham, but there is no fragment of sculpture to help to give them a date; they are only huge irregular basins in the rock, capable of holding from a quarter to two or three millions of gallons each, and for centuries were almost choked with rubbish, till within the last few years our Government has cleared them out and made them available again.

Early the same afternoon we are steaming away

again for Suez, and at midnight pass through the Straits of Babel-mandeb. The little island of Perim divides the straits into two. We pass through the eastern and narrower passage, which is not much more than a mile wide, and by the bright moonlight both the island and the Arabian coast are clearly visible. A few years ago, when the importance of the position of the island first became apparent, and while consuls and envoys were busy discussing to whom it belonged—for it was then uninhabited—the English quietly took possession of it, and are now admitted to have thereby acquired a good title to it. An officer or two and about half a company of troops from Aden are located on it as garrison, and considering that it is perfectly bare, without an inhabitant or a tree, or a blade of grass, or a hill, or water, or, I believe, any animal except rats, and in a climate like a furnace, it must be about as unpleasant a prison to be confined in as well could be found anywhere.

And now we are in the much-dreaded and famous Red Sea. Dreaded it justly is on account of the terrible heat there during the summer months. A captain now on another station told me that when on this line he sometimes lost passengers (most of them invalids, probably) at the rate of one or two every day. Why the heat is so intolerable is not very clear, as the actual temperature by the thermometer is never remarkably high—nothing like so high as in many other places where heat is not much complained of. Fortunately, we are too early in the season to suffer from it, and it is scarcely so hot as before reaching Aden.

The strong north-westerly breeze too, which almost always blows down the sea, meets us and refreshes us. How the navigation was ever performed before the days of steam is a marvel. One of the steamers once fell in with a sailing-ship bound from Aden to Suez, and *seventy-five days out* from the former place, all the crew ill or dead with heat, and only the master and one boy available for duty.

The narrowness of the sea and the dangerous coral reefs which lie on either side, and on which so many fine steamers have been stranded, make all vessels keep to one uniform course straight up the centre of it, out of sight of land on either side. Every day some huge steamer—more often there are two or three—passes with its living freight. For the first time we fully realise what a mighty highway of the world it is. Year by year the long sea-passage by the Cape to India, is less and less followed. Even troops now often take the overland route, and if ever the Suez canal is opened to vessels of large tonnage, the change will be greater still. After centuries of disuse, the old, old road from Europe to India is open again with a hundred times the traffic and importance that it ever had before.

Once only does our vessel pause. A suffering invalid, hoping in vain to reach home alive, has died during the night. In the morning the burial-service is read over the coffin wrapped in a Union-jack, and from a large port on the saloon-deck forward it is lowered gently into the sea; and after scarce five

N

minutes' interval, the engines throb again, and the screw revolves, and the resting-place, unknown and unmarked, is left behind.

On the sixth day from Aden we are in the gulf of Suez. To the east is a flat coast, and beyond is the range of Sinai, scarcely visible. On the west are sandstone cliffs of brilliant red and yellow contrasting exquisitely with the bright blue sky, and lighting up at sunset with the warmest and most gorgeous colours. But we are in Egypt now, and English painters as well as writers have already made the rest of our journey familiar ground, and in their presence it is becoming to be silent. Not that the sights and interests and pleasures of the homeward journey are by any means exhausted yet, or that what is still to be seen loses by comparison with what we have passed. Those who are not pressed for time may stay a week at Cairo, and taking the Southampton instead of the Marseilles route, may also stay at Malta, and during the few hours spent at Gibraltar, walk over the rock and town; and from the vessel's deck as she proceeds see the pretty Spanish and Portuguese coasts for much of the way from thence to Cape St. Vincent.

Melbourne, King George's Sound, Galle, Aden, Suez, the Pyramids, Alexandria, Malta, Gibraltar, Southampton Water. What a list for nine weeks' luxurious travelling! A fresh country about once a week, a fresh continent, almost, once a fortnight!

Truly a P. & O. steamer is a wonderful institution, worthy to take a high place among the unquestionable successes of the last thirty years. Once, in Tasmania, in a remote little bay of D'Entrecasteaux' channel, I came across a man getting his living laboriously by hewing timber in the bush. He told me he had worked in the gang which turned the first sod (or nearly the first) of the new docks in which the first P. & O. ships were cradled. One man sows and toils that another may reap. Few reap so richly, so abundantly, in these days, as those whose time and means enable them to travel on freshly made tracks to see the glory of a new world.

## XV.

### CHANGE OF AIR.

As travelling becomes easier all over the world, an increasing number of people who suffer from English winters are tempted to migrate annually in pursuit of sunshine and a more genial climate. Formerly fewer pleasant places were accessible, and there was comparatively little choice; and as to keep a consumptive person warm through the winter was supposed to be the one thing needful, little attention was paid to other peculiarities of climate. It is only of late years that doctors have become fully alive to the very different effects produced on invalids by much the same temperature in different places. Experience has shown that warmth is by no means the only point to be considered. People who coughed all day and all night at Nice have altogether ceased to cough when they went to Pau, where it was quite as cold. On the other hand, it was found that some people got ill at Pau who were ill nowhere else. Madeira, where it is *never* cold, is going out of repute as a place for consumptive patients; and to the utter astonishment of everybody, it was found that consumptive people who spent a winter in Canada not only did not die immediately but got better.

Climates came to be divided into moist-relaxing, as Madeira, Pisa, and Torquay; dry-relaxing (*sedative*, I believe, is the correct word), as Pau; exciting, as Cannes and Nice; and so on. Doctors became more discriminating in different cases, as far as their geographical knowledge enabled them. But they have something better to do than to go about sniffing the air and observing thermometers and anemometers and hygrometers in half a dozen South-European or Devonshire watering-places. They are obliged for the most part to judge of them from the reports of the local doctors at each place, each of whom is likely to be a believer in his own particular place, and directly interested in making it popular.

And if doctors are compelled to speak with diffidence in distinguishing between European climates, what must their perplexity be when they recommend to their patients, as they often do now, and as I hope they will do more and more, a voyage to Australia? If Cannes has been confounded with Caen, is it surprising if Tasmania should be dimly believed to be one of the West India Islands? What they do know, because they can see that for themselves, is that in cases of threatening consumption, or weakness following an illness, a marvellous change for the better, and often complete cure, is the effect of a voyage round the world. How much of that is due to the sea-air and sea-life, and how much to the land-air and land-life of the Antipodes, they have seldom any means of judging; and still less can they know of the differences in climate between different places in Australasia. An invalid fellow-passenger of ours was furnished with two medical books on the climate of Melbourne, one all praises and encouragement, the other all depreciation and warning. He used to read them alternately in such proportions as to keep his mind in a just balance between hope and fear. Poor fellow! the laudatory book had to come out by itself for a long time, though I think the other appeared now and then when we had been some time in the tropics.

As for the voyage, three months in circumstances inducing the most complete inanition of body and mind of course may, or may not, be desirable. For those who are very weak, either from disease or from overwork of body or brain, I suppose nothing could be more beneficial. Such do not feel the want of bodily exercise and mental occupation which to a more vigorous man is so depressing. It is pleasant to see them, their thin, pinched features gradually relaxing, welcome each day which takes them farther south, discard wrap after wrap, and note down each degree of northern latitude sailed through, till the tropics are reached; where in a temperature seldom varying by day or night beyond a range of from 81° to 85° they breathe the open air throughout the twenty-four hours, with no more exertion than mounting the companion-steps from the berth by the open port in their cabin, to the easy lounging chair under the awning on deck. True, it is a damp heat, and at night it is sometimes soaking wet. Toothache and neuralgia attack you now, if ever they do, and you probably feel limp and lazy and head-achy, and disgusted with everything in the ship except your bath; but the damp does not give cold at sea in the same way as it would on shore, unless anyone is so foolish as to sleep on deck. Nothing can be better for the invalids for the first six or seven weeks of the voyage, and till the tropics are left to the north. But not long after that comes the inevitable and often sudden change. As you get to about 35° or 40° south, the strong westerly winds begin to blow. The ship's course generally touches 45° south, and runs nearly in that latitude for two or three weeks. Doctors and other people at home do not know how much colder 45° south is than 45° north. If, as is pretty sure to happen sooner or later, the wind blows a little from the southward, it may bring sleet and snow with it, and the air may be at 40° or lower for days together, with half a gale of wind blowing all the time to prevent any mistake about how cold it is. It needs no description to give an idea of how dangerous or even fatal this may be to a sick man fresh from his boiling in the tropics, with no fire (probably) in the ship at which he may warm himself, yet for ventilation's sake forced to open window or door from time to time, and to be hustled everywhere, except in bed, by a tempest of draughts. Nor is it possible to escape the cold by timing your departure from England so as to do this part of the voyage in summer. It is more or less cold here all the year round. All things considered, August, September, or October are perhaps the best months to begin the voyage. The English summer is over then, and the coming winter may be cheated.

But much more benefit, I believe, is to be got by invalids from the air of Australia than from the life on board ship. The authorities are now pretty well agreed that, at any rate for consumptive patients, a dry air is the first essential. The statistics, if they are worth anything, go to prove that in England consumption is prevalent or rare in proportion as the soil and situation are light, dry, and high, or, on the other hand, heavy, damp, and low, and that temperature is of secondary importance. Now the Australian air is peculiarly dry — drier than anyone who has never been out of England can well imagine. A new comer from Europe cannot fail to be struck by its exciting, invigorating effect. Considering how great the heat sometimes is, it is astonishing how little it is felt, and how little enervating it is. In the hottest weather the perspiration is absorbed by the air almost immediately, so that the skin is always almost dry. Those who ride about in the heat all day feel it less than those who stay at home. The sun has power even in winter: it is seldom clouded except when rain is actually falling; on the hottest days there is generally a breeze, and indeed the greatest heat comes with the strong hot winds. I never felt any air like it except perhaps that of the Egyptian Desert.

Still it cannot be denied that there are few, if any, places on the mainland where the climate is pleasant all the year round. The way to enjoy the country luxuriously is to migrate with the seasons. Some people indeed like great heat and are all the better for it, and these may do very well in the interior of Victoria or New South Wales all the year round. But except at a few places in Gipp's Land, and elsewhere at a great elevation above the sea, the summer is too hot to be pleasant. The burnt-up grass and vegetation are dismal to look at. The dust is abominable, and the flies sometimes almost amount to a plague. There is no place which is not more or less liable to hot winds, which blow violently from the interior for a day, or two days, at a time, laden with dust, and producing a temperature in the shade often over 100°. These hot winds are not so bad as might be supposed from the degree of heat, but still they are not pleasant; and they cease very suddenly, so that the fall of temperature, especially near the coast, is very great in a short time. I have heard of a fall of 44°, from 106° to 62°, in two hours at Sydney. Near the sea-coast, especially the eastern coast, the air is often cooled by the sea-breezes. At Sydney, for instance, it is not nearly so hot as in the interior. But, strange to say, the cool sea-breeze, instead of being invigorating, is in the long run enervating; and though a stranger at first rejoices in it, it is dreaded by the inhabitants in general, and is the principal cause of the situation of Sydney being less healthy and less bracing than that of most other places in the comparatively temperate parts of Australia. Sydney is, on the whole, to be avoided by those who are fastidious as to climate, except in winter—

that is, in June, July, and August, when it is delightful.

Nor is Melbourne a very pleasant or healthy place in which to spend either winter or summer. It is more agreeable in either spring or autumn. The hot winds of summer and the cold winds of winter are alike disagreeable there. And if, by any chance, there is a day without wind, fog and smoke will sometimes hang over Flinders Street and the low plain stretching towards the bay, making *longo intervallo* an imitation of a London fog. The hospital was crowded with consumptive patients while I was there; but it would not be fair to lay too much of this to the charge of climate. Ill built houses account for much. The comparatively small number of days on which rain falls and the rapidity with which the ground dries make people careless about making their houses waterproof, or draining them properly. Kitchens and servants' rooms are sometimes separated by an open roofless space from the rest of the house, and on rainy days constant wet feet and damp clothes are the consequence. Much illness, too, must be attributed to the bad drainage of Melbourne. A new-comer is at first delighted with the clear running water which is always flowing down the gutters of the principal streets, like Hobson's Conduit at Cambridge. But if he passes by at night his nose informs him that the once limpid stream is neither more nor less than the common sewer of the houses on each side. There are no underground sewers. The rush of water in the hilly streets after heavy rain is so great and sudden that it has been hitherto found impracticable to construct any sewer which would stand against it without bursting. I believe projects are on foot for an effective system of drainage; the Victorians are never sparing of money for public works. But as yet Melbourne is as ill-drained as almost any city I ever saw inhabited by Englishmen, and if cholera or any other bad epidemic ever reached Australia the consequences might be fearful. Even the abundant supply of water, which is such an inestimable advantage in all other respects, makes the evil worse. For before it was obtained, the dry air and especially the hot winds acted as effectual deodorizers by drying up all that was disagreeable, and preventing any effluvium from it. Now there is too much dilution for this to happen, and in parts of the town are to be seen green pools of liquid, poisoning the surrounding air.

Of the climates of Adelaide and of Queensland I cannot speak by experience. From all accounts Adelaide is charming in winter, but in summer even hotter and more burnt up than either Sydney or Melbourne. Brisbane is very hot indeed, almost tropical. But the Darling Downs, high rolling sheep country a couple of hundred miles inland from Brisbane, are said to be in winter charming beyond description; and judging by the experience of a delightful fortnight spent in winter near Scone, two or three hundred miles to the south of them, I can well believe that the winter there affords a type of all that is most charming in Australian air. You have a hot unclouded sun warming you through and through, and raising even the shade temperature to perhaps 70° or 80°; the air never stagnant with the mournful stillness of an English autumn day, but stimulating to exercise, and fresh and bracing beyond what can be conceived in England; boundless open grass country over which you may ride all day on horses that never tire; at night stillness, and perhaps a slight frost, which makes the Squatter's blazing wood-fire grateful; and after a day of perfect bodily enjoyment, you totter off with winking eyes to sleep not the restless sleep of the sickly and feeble, but the sound sleep of the tired and strong.

Of the general attractions of Tasmania I have already spoken, and incidentally of those of its climate. It may be described as midway between the English and the (mainland) Australian, and consequently far pleasanter than either. There are the hot sun, dry air, almost constant breeze, cool nights, sudden changes, and comparative rareness of frost and snow, of Australia; but hot winds are almost unknown there, the sky is more often clouded, and the spring and autumn months are sometimes tempestuous and comparatively cold. The extent of deeply indented sea-coast, and the differences of level in different parts of the country, produce a considerable variety of climate within a small compass. At Hobart Town invalids sometimes suffer from the sea-breeze, which after a hot morning in summer generally blows somewhat keenly in the afternoon, coming up with remarkable regularity at about one o'clock. But a few miles inland its keenness is no longer felt. In summer Tasmania is a delightful refuge from the heat of the continent. The winter there, though colder than that of Victoria, is far warmer, drier, and, above all, lighter and sunnier, than that of any place in England.

I do not wish to disparage European refuges from English winters. But my belief, founded on my own experience, is that in most cases infinitely more benefit is to be obtained by invalids from the Australian than from any European climate. And climate is not the only thing to be considered. What is more depressing, more humiliating to one who seeks to be free, as far as poor humanity may, from the trammels of enfeebled flesh, than the daily routine of a *poitrinaire* at a winter watering-place;—the club room, the tittle-tattle of politics in which he is never likely to take an active part, the still more insipid gossip about other peoples' affairs, the whist by daylight, the weekly weighing to see if flesh is being made or lost? Compare the net result, mental and physical, of a continuance of this sort of life with the rich harvest of memories gathered in from a sight, however limited, of the new southern world. Six months' absence from a profession and from ordinary occupations is in many cases fatal to an immediate resumption of them, and little would really be lost by extending it to a year and a half, which would give ample time for a visit to Australia. The time might be distributed thus: Leaving England by sailing-ship in August or September, and arriving in Melbourne in November or December, a traveller might spend the summer in Tasmania, the autumn in Victoria, and the winter and spring in Queensland and New South Wales, returning to Melbourne some time in the second summer, and sailing thence so as to get home again before the English summer begins. In this way both cold weather and also extreme heat will have been avoided, and two English winters missed. If the whole of the second summer can be spared for going to New Zealand so much the better, or if the mail-steamer's route by way of Galle be taken, a short stay in India during the cool season may be made. Whichever way home is chosen, a much pleasanter voyage may be anticipated if it is begun during the summer months—that is, between the beginning of November and the end of March; for by Cape Horn the cold, by the Red Sea the heat, and round Cape Leuwin and the Cape of Good Hope the adverse winds, become worse as the year advances.

For the reasons already given country life is almost as preferable in regard to health in Australia as it is in England. Those who are not strong enough to travel about much will generally do best to take up their quarters in the country wherever they may have friends or acquaintance. A very slight introduction will procure a very warm welcome everywhere in Australia to any traveller from home. Home has only one meaning there, and long may it keep that meaning. There is no hospitality more readily and kindly proffered and more delightful to accept than that of the Bush. Its simplicity is a pleasant change after the sometimes excessive luxury of English country life. Bed, board, and a horse are at your service; and for sitting-room there is the ample verandah with its wooden or cane lounging-chairs, where air, and light, and sun, will put new strength and vitality into you, if anything will.

Light and sunshine—that is what a weakly man gets in Australia far better than anywhere that I know of in Europe. Perhaps he does not think much about it at the time; but after he is home again, and is groping or shivering through his first English winter, he begins to realize the blessings he has been enjoying.

## XVI.

### A PLEA FOR AUSTRALIAN LOYALTY.

[The *Spectator* of May 23, 1868, contained a letter signed 'An Australian Cynic,' and also an article founded on it, commenting on the extraordinary outburst of excitement and indignation at Sydney occasioned by the attempted assassination of the Duke of Edinburgh, as manifested in the passing of the Treason-Felony Act and in other ways. These manifestations, and the attitude of the Australians generally on the occasion were attributed to a 'starved appetite for rank,' and censured accordingly.

The following Letter was written to endeavour to show that this view of the case was a mistaken and impossible one. The succeeding Letter was an answer to the reply of the *Spectator* that the view of loyalty implied in my first Letter was itself impregnated with 'veiled cynicism.']

YOUR last number contains a letter from 'An Australian Cynic' commenting upon the exhibition of feeling shown in Australia after the attempt to assassinate the Duke of Edinburgh. It also contains an article on the same subject, the writer of which would hardly, I should think, object to being called an English cynic. It seldom happens that English newspapers find space to notice Australia, or that English people care to make themselves acquainted with Australian affairs; and it is unfortunate that when notice is taken of them, the occasion should call for severe not to say contemptuous, censure. Still, let censure fall where censure is due, even though it come under the questionable guise of cynicism. Better too much blame than too little.

But I must confess that to me the spirit which has been shown on this occasion, so far from seeming contemptible, has appeared, on the whole, in the highest degree creditable. I have little hope of being able to bring over you or any of your readers to my way of thinking. Nevertheless, as Australia cannot answer for itself in less than three months, I will endeavour to put the case in the light in which it strikes me.

We Englishmen at home are of all men most devoid of imagination. We spend our lives on soil teeming with tradition, where the very shape or colour of every brick and stone tells its story of the past, and may be a silent but ever-present reminder of some especially honoured friend or hero, some favourite struggle lost or won. But we do not know how much these associations are bound up with us; we cannot tell, till we try, how ill we can dispense with them. I do not believe we have the least idea of the fidelity with which Australians preserve old memories; how tenaciously they cling to their right of inheritance in the history of the past. At first it may be that an emigrant is altogether engrossed with the occupations of the moment. He must get his bread; he must strike his roots into the new soil; he has no time to sit down and think. But as he grows older, when he finally makes up his mind to make the new country his home, old memories and old attachments return with immense force. An old weather-beaten settler, who after a life spent in hardships at last sees his children growing up about him in prosperity and comfort, will look at them proudly, yet half sadly, knowing that he has within him an inheritance which he can transmit to them only in part, doubting whether after all a dinner of herbs amongst the old scenes and the old traditions, sustaining (so he fancies) the old beliefs, is not better than a stalled ox without them. No one who has not experienced Australian hospitality can imagine the jealous care which they take of a chance visitor from England, how distressed and almost angry a settler will be if a visitor, although an utter stranger, puts up at an inn instead of going to his house. And as you talk to him, the chances are he will speak sadly, even bitterly, of the carelessness, the indifference of people at home to their Australian Colonies. They do not know even by name one colony from another. Melbourne and Sydney are set down as places where a revolver is as necessary as an umbrella in London; their populations as composed mainly of convicts, runaways from Europe, dishonest demagogues, or merchants who care to remain only till they have made their fortunes. But what he will complain of most bitterly is that a school has grown up in England which says, 'Let the Colonies go. All we want of them is wool and gold. All they want of us is a market. What we both want is wealth.

We can get this as well separate as together, perhaps better. Traditions, loyalty to the throne, willingness to share danger as well as security, war as well as peace, with the old country—all this is sentimental rubbish. 'We have almost got rid of this sort of thing at home, they must have quite got rid of it at the Antipodes.'

This, I believe, is false slander. As such, I believe it has been felt, and felt keenly, by the vast majority of Australians. Can you, then, wonder that when the news came that the Queen was sending out one of the Princes, not selfishly, for his own benefit or for that of the Crown, still less to confer any mere *material* benefit on the Australians, it came to them like a chance offered to a maligned man to clear himself from a false charge—like light thrown on a dark place? And so, when the Duke, after weeks and months of expectation, at last arrived, it did not matter whether they did or did not find him all that they thought an English Prince would be and ought to be; it did not matter if he disliked politics, was bored by balls and 'functions,' was indifferent to the beauty of the country. They refused to look a gift horse in the mouth. He was the Queen's son; that was enough. They would do him all possible honour, and so prove that they were loyal Englishmen, and cared for Queen and country as well as gold and wool.

And when the news came that the Duke had been shot at and wounded on their own shores, every one in a strange way seemed to take it to heart, to be struck with shame and dismay, as though he himself were in part guilty of the crime. The terror of having to bear, as a body, the guilt of one wretched man excited them almost beyond belief. At Hobart Town—distant as Tasmania is from the scene of the occurrence (I quote from a hurriedly written letter just received)—

'A meeting was convened within an hour of the arrival of the news by telegraph; it was attended by every class and sect in the community. The large town hall could not contain the assemblage; they therefore gathered outside. The first proceeding, before any resolution, was to call for the substitution of the Union flag for the municipal one. Then, regardless of order, but with the order inspired by a common sentiment, the vast crowd struck up the National Anthem. The effect drew tears from many eyes—the *effect* in part, the *earnestness* with which, under the circumstances, the Anthem was given forth by those who joined in it, melted them into weakness. And a second time in the course of the proceedings the same *irregularity* was indulged in, without its being possible for any one to say that anything irregular was done—the ordinary and decorous modes of expressing popular feeling were insufficient to give utterance to that by which all were *possessed*. We burned with loyalty to the Crown and country, intensified by shame and indignation that the act of one bad man had made it necessary that we should wipe away reproach or suspicion from us. I am not guilty of exaggeration when I tell you that the news of what had been done by O'Farrell made many persons *ill* amongst us. . . . . . I dwell upon this subject, for to this moment it, more than any other public one, agitates the minds of the people—but having done so for this simple reason, let me ask you, as a recent visitant, to do something in our vindication. We are English — that is, national—in our sentiments, and not as the result of calculation, but simply because we have not ceased to be and to feel as Englishmen. Our Tasmanianism is an accident of no more qualifying influence upon our feelings in what relates to the honour and integrity of the mother country, than the circumstance might have of being Kentish men.'

Strange words these, to come, as they do, not from a hot-headed boy, but from a cool, experienced politician, a reader of solid books, a grave paterfamilias, a hater of public meetings, who, when the Duke was in Hobart Town, was ready to escape into the country, rather than face the fuss and bustle and (to him) annoyance of festivities and 'functions.' And column after column of the Australian papers tell the same story. I do not believe, since the news of Waterloo came to England, that any body of Englishmen have been heated to so intense and so unanimous a pitch of enthusiasm. Nor would it be possible to name any such manifestation more unmixed with selfishness. For ostentatious loyalty there are no rewards or honours in Australia, whatever there may be for ostentatious democracy. I am no believer in the *Vox populi vox Dei* doctrine. But surely such an outburst as this is a phenomenon at least worthy of patient examination. What is to be said of the discernment or of the charity of a writer who can dismiss it with a passing sneer as 'the starved appetite for rank'?

How 'An Australian Cynic' can say that there is 'not a tittle of evidence that a single colonist of New South Wales, native or immigrant, has ever harboured a thought of treason' I am at a loss to conceive. I know little or nothing of what has been going on lately in New South Wales. But it is not a year since a

Roman Catholic chaplain of one of the convict establishments had to be dismissed for preaching Fenianism to the prisoners; to say nothing of the original statement made by O'Farrell himself, which it is as difficult to disprove as to prove. I doubt if the absurdities and extravagances of the Treason-Felony Act are worth the pains 'An Australian Cynic' has taken to criticize them. The Judges are not likely to allow the Act to be enforced in an improper manner. Its intention is obvious enough, and the blunders will probably prove to be harmless surplusage. Nobody expects much legislative wisdom from a House constituted as the Lower House of New South Wales is. Nor is the Upper House likely to be much better, since it consists, not of members chosen by a superior constituency, like the Victorian Upper House, but of nominees ostensibly of the Governor, but in reality of successive administrations. Nor ought we at home to be too ready to ridicule their legislation, when we recollect that it is we who are responsible for their Constitution. It was we who at a time of transition and excitement in Australia allowed our Parliament and Ministers to pitchfork out to New South Wales a rash, ill-considered scheme, from which, in the opinion of many, the colony has been suffering ever since.

'An Australian Cynic' complains of the newspapers and the public at Sydney for not being more interested about a murder of five people which has been committed in the interior. Does he mean to imply that the police are supine in the matter, and need stimulus, or that the existing law is inadequate to meet the case? If not, why ought such a topic to be enlarged upon? Ought all bloodshed to provoke an amount of discussion exactly in proportion to the number of lives lost? Murder, unfortunately, is too old and too common a crime not to have been provided against as far as it is possible to do so. Fenianism, when it assumes the form of a conspiracy for the wholesale assassination of the most prominent persons in the State, is a new crime and requires new precautions. I suppose there must be a sense (since so many hold to the dogma) in which all men may be said to be equal, though I must confess I never could discover any—never yet having seen such a phenomenon as even two men who could in any sense of the word be called equal. But the common sense of all communities acknowledges that the lives of some persons are (to take the lowest ground) infinitely more valuable to the State than those of others, and when for this reason exposed to special danger they require to be specially protected.

Political assassination is a new crime in England in our days. But if we go back to the days of Queen Elizabeth, we may be reminded of conspiracies not unlike the worst manifestations of Fenianism, which were met by our ancestors in a spirit not altogether unlike that which has just been shown by their descendants in Australia.

## XVII.

### LOYALTY AND CYNICISM.

\*      \*      \*      \*      \*

PERSONALLY I do plead guilty to holding the belief or doctrine to hold which you call 'veiled cynicism.' But I beg you will not suppose that I am asserting that the late demonstration of the Australians necessarily implied that *they* hold it, or that their loyalty as a people was not wider and more comprehensive than any particular phase of it which may specially present itself to me or to any one person. In the following remarks I shall speak only in my own defence, and try to lift my 'veil,' so that it may be seen whether what is behind is, or is not, cynicism.

I accept the definition of cynicism which you give in your first paragraph. But I will add another, and a strictly etymological one. A cynic is a man who treats a deep-seated reasonable belief, or a fair argument, in a dog-like manner, as if it were a mere dog's howl; one who vouchsafes only a kick or an imprecation to what he ought to listen to with patience, and answer (if he disagrees) with argument. A sham belief and an utterly worthless argument *ought* to get only kicks and imprecations; to treat them otherwise would be priggishness. It is a critic's business and difficulty to discover the right path between these two pitfalls. With all respect to the *Spectator*, I venture to express my opinion that not only in its recent article on the New South Wales Treason-Felony Act, but again and again in speaking of matters pertaining to the Crown and its relation to the people, it has fallen into the pitfall of cynicism, and (unwittingly, of course) written what has jarred painfully on the convictions of not a few amongst its readers.

To define these convictions adequately in general terms is almost impossible. I do not know how to do so without entering upon theological questions too deep for me, and which I would rather have avoided. I do not know how better to express my own conviction than by saying that I do in a very real sense believe in the 'divine right of kings;' not of course in the sense of the High Church party of the seventeenth century; more nearly, perhaps, in that of the eminently national and protestant party, which in the latter part of the sixteenth century relied upon the doctrine as the truest and strongest bulwark against Rome and Spain. I believe in the institution of hereditary monarchy as a divine idea, imparted to mankind, and answering to true and healthy instincts implanted in them—like in kind, if differing in degree, to the institution of a priesthood or clergy. Nations may reject it if they please. In so doing they are simply rejecting a proffered blessing, just as all of us are rejecting blessings every day. The non-juring Bishops and their followers brought discredit on the doctrine by their unphilosophical perversion of it. They forgot that a dynasty, like an individual Church, may become so degraded by the unworthiness of its members as to receive its condemnation, as did the dynasties of Saul and of Ahab.

The history of Europe from the middle ages to the present time teems with instances of intense attachment to hereditary, or quasi-hereditary, monarchy, often breaking out in the strangest and most unaccountable way, and in the teeth of the bitterest tyranny. For instance, it would be hard, even in the thirteenth century, to find a monarch who had inflicted more suffering and bloodshed on his subjects than Frederick Barbarossa inflicted on the Lombards. He was of a different race, too, and spoke a different language. Yet when his power had been broken under the walls of Alessandria, and he found himself face to face with a mass of enemies from whom escape was impossible, and whom to attack was certain defeat, he could calmly pitch his camp in the presence of their armed hosts, in the confidence (which the event justified) that in spite of all they would still acknowledge him as their Sovereign, and that his life and liberty were safe in their hands.\*

What is more remarkable in the death scenes of all the religious and political martyrs or sufferers, from

---

\* Sismondi, *Ital. Rep.* vol. ii. ch. xi. p. 212.

Sir Thomas More to Sir Walter Raleigh, staunch as they were to the end each to his religious creed, than the eagerness with which they repelled as an insult every imputation of disloyalty to the Throne? And yet at least two out of the five Sovereigns who reigned were as despicable as a Sovereign can be. How incredible to us seems the picture of the House of Commons, in the succeeding reign, with many of its members *in tears* of shame, that the Throne, and they with it, should be so degraded by its occupant!

One hears of speeches so absorbing or exciting that men hold their breath to listen. I used to think this was only a figure of speech; but it happened to me once, and once only, to find it a literal fact. The Bishop of New Zealand was preaching at St. Mary's (Cambridge), which was crammed with undergraduates. The subject was the Queen's supremacy. He described shortly and tersely the 'shaking of the nations,' the abject condition, danger, or dethronement of the Sovereigns of Europe in 1848. But when he came to our own Queen, and her tranquil security in the midst of the storm, he used no words of his own; he simply quoted the text, 'He took a little child, and set her in the midst.' It was then that for, perhaps, ten seconds every hearer held his breath. The silence was, from its intensity, more startling, less capable of being forgotten, than any sound I ever heard.

Now, I do not mean to say that the Lombards, on

the occasion referred to, acted like patterns of magnanimous loyalty. I am not quite sure that they were not, considering all the circumstances, rather fools for their pains. Nor do I mean to say that the extraordinary effect of the Bishop's words was due *solely* to the intrinsic truth and value of the idea suggested, or to the eagerness with which his hearers' instincts went out to meet it, and not in part to the perfect rhetoric in which it was clothed. But I say that there is a vein of gold in the substratum of all these incidents, and of hundreds of similar ones, which refuses to float away upon any such superficial explanation—a metal the taking away of which would leave poor humanity sadly impoverished.

Doubtless an hereditary Sovereign is not the only possible object of loyalty. There may be loyalty to a President, to a 'House,' even, I suppose, to a shadowy, ever-changing idea such as a Constitution. Mr. Carlyle has taught us, to a greater extent than we can well estimate, how to choose our heroes. But does he not fall short of entirely satisfying us, because his conception of a hero is indissolubly bound up with mere force of will and power of mind? Like Mr. Carlyle's heroes, the Presidents of Republics and the leaders of great parties are of necessity men of iron will, muscular intellect, and, it may safely be added, invincible digestions. Why should we narrow our field of choice and contract our storehouse of types of rulers within this small class? Why should we honour a man for his natural ability any more than we honoured Tom Sayers or Lola Montez for their strength and beauty? Does not the Bishop's quotation suggest a deliverance from this perplexity? May not our heroes be sometimes chosen for us? In the long lists of the Sovereigns of past times have we not a St. Louis as well as a Francis I., an Edward VI. as well as a Henry V., a Margaret of Navarre as well as a Maria Theresa, an Elizabeth of Hungary as well as an Elizabeth of England? Can even these few types be found amongst Presidents of Republics, or could they be selected and enthroned by any form of suffrage, universal or other?

Therefore it is (as it seems to me) that hereditary sovereignty naturally commends itself to men's truest and deepest instincts as supplying and enlisting more true types of humanity, as more readily suggesting the idea of perfect humanity and a perfect ruler, as more symbolic of human-divine government, than any other kind of rule. The remembrance of sovereigns at once bad and feeble soon slips out of history. The memory of the good, were they strong or feeble, remains a rich ever-accumulating treasure to humanity, adding type to type, building up in all reverent minds an ever loftier ideal of government, which is not the less precious for being so imperfectly realized.

A mere leader, however great, whether priest, poet, or politican, represents his own type, his own class, or his own party. Homage to him can seldom, if ever, be unanimous; it is ever on the brink of degenerating into party-spirit and sectarianism. A Sovereign represents the strong and the weak, the great and the insignificant, the man with one talent and the man with seven, the traditions of the past and the ideas of the present. A Sovereign is the only possible representative of the *whole* nation. I may be wrong, but I think that the Australians, consciously or unconsciously, found this to be true.

LONDON: PRINTED BY
SPOTTISWOODE AND CO., NEW-STREET SQUARE
AND PARLIAMENT STREET

www.ingramcontent.com/pod-product-compliance
Lightning Source LLC
Chambersburg PA
CBHW021843230426
43669CB00008B/1060